Practical Guide to
Project-Based Learning

Practical Guide to Project-Based Learning

Mun Wai Ho
Republic Polytechnic, Singapore

Mark Brooke
National University of Singapore

WS Education

NEW JERSEY · LONDON · SINGAPORE · BEIJING · SHANGHAI · HONG KONG · TAIPEI · CHENNAI · TOKYO

Published by

WS Education, an imprint of
World Scientific Publishing Co. Pte. Ltd.
5 Toh Tuck Link, Singapore 596224
USA office: 27 Warren Street, Suite 401-402, Hackensack, NJ 07601
UK office: 57 Shelton Street, Covent Garden, London WC2H 9HE

Library of Congress Cataloging-in-Publication Data
Names: Ho, Mun Wai. | Brooke, Mark, author.
Title: Practical guide to project-based learning / Mun Wai Ho,
   Republic Polytechnic, Singapore, Mark Brooke, NUS, Singapore.
Description: New Jersey : World Scientific, 2017. | Includes bibliographical references.
Identifiers: LCCN 2017002274| ISBN 9789813202191 | ISBN 9789813202207 (pbk)
Subjects: LCSH: Project method in teaching.
Classification: LCC LB1027.43 .H6 2017 | DDC 371.3/6--dc23
LC record available at https://lccn.loc.gov/2017002274

British Library Cataloguing-in-Publication Data
A catalogue record for this book is available from the British Library.

Copyright © 2017 by World Scientific Publishing Co. Pte. Ltd.

All rights reserved. This book, or parts thereof, may not be reproduced in any form or by any means, electronic or mechanical, including photocopying, recording or any information storage and retrieval system now known or to be invented, without written permission from the publisher.

For photocopying of material in this volume, please pay a copying fee through the Copyright Clearance Center, Inc., 222 Rosewood Drive, Danvers, MA 01923, USA. In this case permission to photocopy is not required from the publisher.

Desk Editor: Shreya Gopi

Typeset by Stallion Press
Email: enquiries@stallionpress.com

CONTENTS

Foreword   xi
Foreword   xiii
Acknowledgement   xv
Preface   xvii
About the Authors   xxi

Chapter 1   **Curricular Objectives of 'Project Work'**   1

    1.1 What is 'Project Work' in the curriculum of tertiary education?   2
    1.2 What are the differences between a dissertation, thesis, project report or an extended essay?   3
    1.3 What are the curricular objectives of PW   3
    1.4 Who are the main stakeholders in a project and what are their roles and responsibilities?   5
    1.5 When should the industry seek to collaborate with tertiary institutions to undertake projects? Are there alternative approaches?   8
    1.6 Can a lecturer who is not a domain expert of the project topic perform the role of the academic supervisor for the project effectively?   9
    1.7 What should be the appropriate duration of PW?   10

1.8	Is PW just another assignment given to students?	12
1.9	Must all PWs be about research? Must they be industry-linked?	13
1.10	What are the differences between research-based and practice-based projects?	15
1.11	Are research-based PWs more prestigious than practice-based PWs?	17
1.12	Must practice-based PWs be done in collaboration with the industry?	18
1.13	What is Design Thinking?	18
1.14	Must PWs lead to publication of papers in academic journals?	22
1.15	How to write a project proposal?	23

Chapter 2 Structure of the Report/Dissertation/Thesis   29

2.1	What is the structure of PW report, which may also be known as a dissertation or a thesis?	30
2.2	What is a publishable paper?	32
2.3	How long should the PW deliverable be in terms of word count?	33
2.4	Are there conventions to follow in terms of formatting?	34
2.5	What are the commonly used citations and referencing styles?	38
2.6	What is an Abstract? Is an Abstract the same as a Synopsis?	48
2.7	What should be included in the Introduction?	49
2.8	What should be included in the literature review?	49

2.9 What is a Conceptual Framework of Inquiry? 51
2.10 What is the Methodology Chapter for? 53
2.11 What are some specific topics that should be included in the Methodology Chapter? 55
2.12 What are the theoretical underpinnings of the methodology applied? 56
2.13 What is mixed methods and triangulation? 58
2.14 What should be included in the chapter on data collation and analysis? 60
2.15 What should be included in the Conclusion Chapter? 61

Chapter 3 Techniques in Reference Sourcing and Styles of Academic Writing 63

3.1 Why must PW involve sourcing for data and information? 64
3.2 What are useful strategies for finding sources? 66
3.3 How can information about a topic be collated and annotated systematically? 70
3.4 What are useful strategies for mapping out the big picture? 72
3.5 How should sources be used in academic writing? 75
3.6 What are some guiding principles for effective academic writing? 77
3.7 What is grammar and how is it important in academic writing? 78
3.8 What is cohesion in academic writing? 78

3.9 How do I construct a noun group and what is nominalization?   85
3.10 Should I use active or passive voice in academic writing?   89
3.11 What is Subject-verb agreement?   92
3.12 What is hedging?   95
3.13 What is affixation?   96
3.14 How do I punctuate academic English correctly?   101
3.15 Where can useful sources to develop academic writing be found?   105

Chapter 4 Selection of Methodology   107

4.1 How to consider the choice of methodology of a project?   108
4.2 What are quantitative and qualitative analysis?   112
4.3 What should be presented in an analysis with descriptive statistics?   113
4.4 What is hypothesis testing?   123
4.5 What are correlation and regression analysis?   128
4.6 What is Structural Equation modeling?   133
4.7 What are the commonly used qualitative analytical methods?   134
4.8 What is a case study?   134
4.9 How to do interview in data collection?   136
4.10 How to do observation in data collection?   137
4.11 What is coding?   139
4.12 What is SWOT analysis?   140
4.13 What is the Boston Consulting Group Matrix   141

	4.14 What is reliability and validity and how are these terms viewed in qualitative research methodology?	142
Chapter 5	**Assessment**	**145**
	5.1 What is the difference between formative and summative assessment?	146
	5.2 How can students participate in formative peer assessment?	146
	5.3 How should summative assessment be conducted?	148
	5.4 Does the assessment rubric need to be different for research-based and practice-based projects respectively?	152
	5.5 What is a poster presentation and how to prepare for this?	153
	5.6 What is the 'Pecha Kucha' presentation format?	155
Chapter 6	**Project Management**	**159**
	6.1 Is it necessary for interim reports to be submitted in addition to the final report? If these are needed, how can these be organized?	160
	6.2 Is it necessary for PW to have regular scheduled project meetings?	160
	6.3 What is a Gantt chart?	161
	6.4 What if the project is too big and it cannot be structured within one PW and be completed in a Semester or an Academic Year?	163

6.5 Can a project be assigned to more than one candidate or groups of students? 164

Chapter 7 Ethics Declaration 167

7.1 Why is there a need to declare 'ethics' in research or project work? 168
7.2 What are the key principles to consider in administering ethics? 168
7.3 Do the requirements for the declaration of ethics differ in different institutions and in different countries? 170
7.4 Is there any situation when an ethics declaration is not required? 170
7.5 What does the process for ethics declaration entail? 171

Bibliography 173

Annex A   Project Schedule 177

Annex B   Project Proposal Sample 181

Annex C   Project Gantt Chart 187

Epilogue 189

FOREWORD

Lee Kwok Cheong, PBM, BBM
Hon DSc (London), Hon DBus (RMIT), Hon FSCS
Adjunct Professor (UniSIM)
Chief Executive Officer, SIM Global Education

Michael Koh, PPA(P)
PhD, B.Sc (Hons), PGCE
Deputy Principal (Academic Affairs)
Republic Polytechnic Singapore

Wu Siew Mei
PhD (NUS), MA (Monash), BA (Hons) (NUS), DipEd (NUS)
Associate Professor, Director, Centre of English
Language Communication
National University of Singapore

Project-based learning may be known by various names. Fundamentally, it entails solving a problem in a methodical way, and reporting the endeavor and the outcome so as to contribute towards knowledge creation and/or improvements in practice in the real world. Indeed, it is an integral and an increasingly important part of the curriculum in polytechnics and universities as well as the International Baccalaureate (IB) and the Integrated Programme (IP) in Singapore.

Hence, this book is a timely addition to the repertoire of resources to help not only students, but also supervisors from the academia and the industry to collaborate within the context of project-based learning. In fact, this book has become even more pertinent with the increased emphasis on linking learning in the academia to practice in the real world.

We would like to congratulate Mun Wai and Mark who have leveraged on their experience in observing, reflecting, and collaborating with the industry, fellow academics as well as supervising students to put together this book. In the true sense of problem solving, this book has been written and organized with a practical approach by discussing the various topics as a series of questions and answers. This will allow the readers to zoom in on the specific issue they would like to seek clarification on. Nevertheless, it is also highly readable should the reader like to read it sequentially as the chapters have been arranged logically within the thought process of problem solving and writing the project dissertations. Furthermore, it is also written in plain English which makes it universally readable especially for uses in Singapore and Asia.

We appreciate the work of Mun Wai and Mark, and commend it to those seeking knowledge as well as those endeavoring in the mission to educate and nurture the leaders of tomorrow.

FOREWORD

Nicholas Walliman
PhD, Dipl. Arch
Senior Lecturer, Faculty of Technology, Design and Environment
Oxford Brookes University
United Kingdom

David Ho Kim Hin
Hon DLitt, PhD; MPhil, B.Sc (Hons)
Associate Professor, School of Design and Environment
National University of Singapore

Project-based learning is increasingly being used to introduce practical applications of the theoretical information delivered to students in a wide range of subjects. Students relish the opportunity to test out their newly acquired knowledge in the real world but need a strong framework in order to maximize the benefits of this form of learning. Industry collaborators also appreciate the chance to encounter young entrepreneurs and to help them harness their skills in business relevant contexts. Academic staff see industry linked projects as an ideal method of bringing relevance to their teaching for the career development of their students.

In light of these potential advantages there is a need for rigorous planning of project-based learning to ensure that all parties can benefit from the process. Using a multi-stakeholder approach, Ho Mun Wai and Mark Brooke examine the advantages of Project Work and describe the issues involved in sufficient detail to be used as a practical guide to designing, implementing, and assessing project work. The complexity of managing expectations of all the stakeholders is carefully considered by taking into account reasons for engagement, roles allotted, formulation of aims, research methods, ethical issues, project management, types of deliverables and assessment of the outcomes.

This book is an essential guide for academics and industrialists who wish to engage students in project-based learning initiatives. Clearly written and comprehensive, it provides all the advice necessary to devise and manage the diverse components of student projects, which, if followed, will result in valuable learning outcomes and enjoyable and enriching experience for students, teachers and industry collaborators.

ACKNOWLEDGEMENT

We would to thank our superiors and colleagues at the Republic Polytechnic and National University of Singapore who have supported and assisted in one way or another. We are indebted to the industry collaborators with whom we have the privilege to work as well as the students we have taught who have given us the inspiration to embark on this endeavor. We would also like to thank our families for their wonderful support and encouragement. Last but not least, we are especially grateful to Dr Lee Kwok Cheong, Dr Michael Koh, Professor Wu Siew Mei, Professor David Ho and Dr Nicholas Walliman who have contributed the Forewords as well as to Shreya Gopi from World Scientific for her professional support and guidance in the publication of this book.

PREFACE

Ho Mun Wai
Republic Polytechnic, Singapore
Email: ho_mun_wai@rp.edu.sg

Mark Brooke
National University of Singapore
Email: elcmb@nus.edu.sg

It is common for undergraduate programs in universities to include a Final Year Project (FYP) based on which students will need to write a thesis or a dissertation. Beyond universities, such FYP or Project Work (PW) in general has also become a common feature in the curriculum in junior colleges, polytechnics and other similar tertiary institutions. Indeed, in the increasingly popular International Baccalaureate (IB) program as well as the Integrated Programme (IP) in Singapore, PW is becoming an increasingly important element of their pedagogical philosophy.

But, what is PW? Must it be about research? Must it be done in collaboration with the industry? Should it involve the use of sophisticated statistics? Can organizing an event or the fabrication of a device fulfill the curriculum requirements of PW? How do projects in natural and social sciences differ? How much time and academic weight should PW entail? What is the role of the academic supervisor, the industry supervisor, and the student? Can a teacher or an educator who does not have substantive subject matter expertise of the project perform the role of the academic supervisor for the project? These are some of the issues educators and students may encounter from time to time.

It is important that the above issues are addressed comprehensively prior to the commencement of the PW so that the learning experience of students can be optimized and the desired educational outcome can be achieved. Therefore, it is intended that this book shall serve primarily as a practical reference for instructors, academic and industry supervisors to design, structure and supervise their PWs so that they will serve the desired curricular objectives as well as that of the various stakeholders.

As a secondary objective, this book is also intended to serve as a companion to help students navigate through their PWs. Hopefully, such experience will motivate and help prepare them for further studies and fruitful careers in the future as professionals, managers or researchers. While a lot of the discussions in the book seem to be approached from the perspective of academic supervisors, students will also be able to benefit from such insights by having a better understanding of the context and rationale why the academic requirements of the PW are structured one way or the other.

PW essentially entails problem solving. Thus, it is a very apt academic platform for the operationalization of the Project-Based Learning (PBL) pedagogy. A central theme of the PBL pedagogy is to inculcate an inquiring mind towards understanding a phenomenon and applying such understanding towards solving a problem or investigating a phenomenon. In line with the true spirit of PBL, this book is therefore structured as a series of questions and responses. Readers can read this book sequentially. Alternatively, they can also use this book as a companion for their journey through their PW. They can do so by going to the content to look for the specific matter of interest and thereafter, look for the discussions therein. Accordingly, this book is not intended to be a textbook on research methods or statistical analysis. Readers are recommended to consult the specialized literature on research methodology and statistical analysis to augment their technical competency in this regard.

ABOUT THE AUTHORS

Ho Mun Wai

Dr Ho Mun Wai received his BE and MSc from the National University Singapore (NUS), MBA from the Lancaster University, and Doctor of Business Administration from the University of South Australia. He has also attended the NUS Senior Management Programme, the Stanford-NUS Executive Programme, and the Harvard-NUS Executive Programme on negotiation. Mun Wai has served as Vice-Dean (Admin) in the School of Medicine in the NUS, as well as in various academic roles in the ITE, and the Republic Polytechnic. Mun Wai's education portfolio include forging industry collaborations, such as in structuring internships, formulating continuing education and training programmes, and implementing various industry linked projects. Beyond the academia, he has also helmed various corporate functions including knowledge management, corporate planning, business analysis and relationship management in the Singapore Sports Council and the JTC Corp. Mun Wai is a Fellow of the Singapore Institute of Arbitrators (FSIArb), and a Chartered Member of the Chartered Institute of Logistics and Transport (CMILT). He has published in international peer reviewed journals and presented at international conferences.

Mark Brooke

Dr Mark Brooke is a Lecturer at the Centre for English Language Communication (CELC), part of the National University of Singapore (NUS). He is also Associate Editor of the CELC's online journal English Language Teaching World Online as well as several other internationally reviewed journals in English language teaching. Mark has published in the field of applied linguistics, particularly Content and Language Integrated Learning, and in the field of the Sociology of Sport. Prior to joining NUS, Mark worked as a Senior Teaching Fellow at the Hong Kong Institute of Education and as a Lecturer at City University of Hong Kong. He has also worked as a language instructor in tertiary or adult education in France, Italy, the UK and mainland China. Mark holds a Doctorate in Education from the University of Durham, UK; an MSc from Aston University (UK) in Teaching English for Specific Purposes; a post-graduate Diploma in TESOL from Trinity College London, UK; and a Masters in English Literature with a focus on Critical Theory; and a Diploma in Advanced French Studies from Bordeaux University in France. He also holds a BA (hons) from the University of Sunderland in the UK.

CHAPTER 1

CURRICULAR OBJECTIVES OF 'PROJECT WORK'

After reading this chapter, you will be able to:

— *Design a project for academic inquiry.*

— *Decide if a project should be research-based or practice-based.*

— *Consider if a project should involve industry collaboration.*

— *Write a project proposal.*

1.1 What is 'Project Work' in the curriculum of tertiary education?

Project Work (PW) is a common feature in the curriculum in junior colleges, polytechnics and universities. Indeed, in the increasingly popular International Baccalaureate (IB) program as well as the Integrated Programme (IP) in Singapore, PW is even central to the pedagogical philosophy.

PW may be done through various platforms or named in different ways. Some examples of these include:

— Final Year Projects (FYP),

— Final Year Thesis (FYT),

— Final Year Dissertation (FYD),

— Term Paper (TP),

— Extended Essay (EE), as in the IB program, or simply

— Project Work (PW) as in the General Certificate of Education (GCE) 'A' level curriculum.

For the purpose of this book, the generic terms of Project Work (PW) or simply 'project' are used interchangeably to refer to various types of projects offered in tertiary education.

It is common for PW to be a curriculum requirement in the final year of a course of study. What this means is that PW is directed at the application of knowledge and competencies gained in the earlier years of studies in an integrated manner towards addressing an issue of interest.

1.2 What are the differences between a dissertation, thesis, project report or an extended essay?

In American universities, a dissertation is the work that is submitted to earn a doctorate degree, while a thesis is submitted to fulfill part of the requirements for a master's or bachelor's degree. However, in the British context, the reverse would apply. Hence, it is not surprising that the usage of these terms can be confusing.

Nevertheless, a common thread of their descriptions is that they entail an endeavor in research or problem solving in the academic context.

In continuation from Section 1.1 earlier, the discussions in this book will refer to them generically as dissertation, Project Work report or simply PW report. While the PW reports submitted for the different levels of studies in the universities, polytechnics, colleges or high schools differ in terms of the expectations of length, rigor and originality, the basic principles upon which they should be constructed are similar as discussed in this book.

1.3 What are the curricular objectives of PW?

Project-based learning (PBL) is an approach that seeks to organize learning around projects. Projects, as compared to issues in specific modules, are usually characterized by their multi-dimensional nature.

Accordingly, PW is directed at the application of knowledge and competencies gained in the earlier years of studies in an integrated manner towards addressing an issue of interest. They provide the platform to engage students in investigative activities, problem solving, decision making, and design. They also provide opportunities for students to work relatively independently over extended periods of time (Thomas, 2000).

The key aspect of a PW is the applied and integrated nature. It should be student-driven, involve students in constructive investigation, realistic and be differentiated from traditional didactic teaching in the classrooms.

Specifically, PW can be directed at achieving two equally important objectives (Figure 1.1):

a. Process: Develop and test the problem-solving skills in addressing a set of research questions or finding solutions to a set of problems in practice.

b. Content: Enhance and test competencies in a specialization discipline. Students are to demonstrate that they are able to draw from the subjects or modules they have learnt earlier and apply them in the context of the projects they work on.

It is alright that the balance between the two objectives may differ from project to project. What is important is that the expectations must be discussed and clarified among the supervisor, student and the external collaborator as far as possible before and during the course of the project.

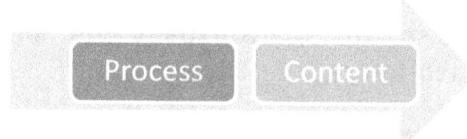

Figure 1.1 Twin curricular objectives of PBL.

1.4 Who are the main stakeholders in a project and what are their roles and responsibilities?

A project will entail at least two parties, namely, the academic supervisor and the student. They have distinct roles.

It is important for these to be clarified and mutually understood prior to the commencement of the project such that the student will be able to optimize his or her learning and that the other objectives of the academic supervisor can also be met.

At times, a project may also be undertaken in conjunction with an industry collaborator. In this case, the problem may entail addressing an issue defined by the industry collaborator. In such instances, the project will involve a third party and the academic supervisor will have additional duties (Figure 1.2).

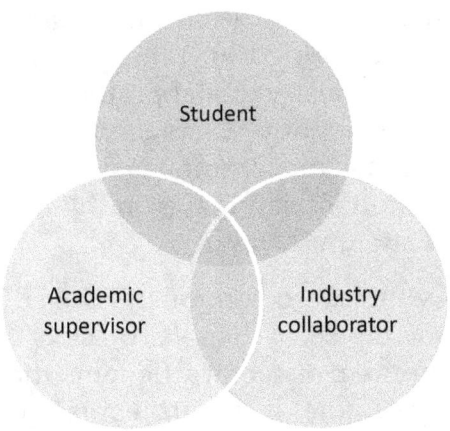

Figure 1.2 Key stakeholders in a project.

In general, the roles of each party are suggested below:

Student:

— Take full ownership for self-directed learning in order to complete the project.

— Should not rely on the supervisor to solve the problem for him. The supervisor's primary role is to provide guidance and facilitation.

The academic supervisor:

— Ensure the design of the project is appropriate for the level of studies of the student and doable within the constraints of time and other resources.

— Provide adequate and appropriate intervention to ensure the project progresses in accordance to plans.

— Not to take over and complete the project on behalf of the student.

— In an industry-linked project, the academic supervisor should also have formed an understanding or an agreement with the industry collaborator on the scope and design of the project prior to its start. This is important so that when the semester commences and the student comes on board, the student can focus on the substantive matter of the project straight away.

— Specifically with regard to industry-linked projects, it will be a cause of concern if the project is affected due to delays or commercial factors beyond the control of the students, for example, if the project is for the students to organize an event for an external industry collaborator, but this event has to be cancelled midway due to the change of plan of the industry collaborator. If and when such things happen, the academic supervisor will have to intervene and prioritize on finding solutions that will allow the student to complete the project and fulfill the academic requirements.

The industry supervisor:

— Be familiar with the academic perspectives on why the project is structured as a PW with industry collaboration.

— One of the critical factors necessary for the successful completion of industry-linked PW (Figure 1.3) is that the industry collaborators should also be concerned with providing the learning experience to the students rather than treating the students as a mere resource or outsourced contractors. Thus, it is advisable that the industry collaborators ensure that they are able to align their intentions with that of the academic institutions, which is to educate and nurture the students. If not, they should consider alternatives of engaging consultants or contractors on a commercial basis.

Figure 1.3 Industry-linked PW provides opportunities to achieve win–win outcome for the academic institution, industry collaborator and the students within a nurturing context.

1.5 When should the industry seek to collaborate with tertiary institutions to undertake projects? Are there alternative approaches?

Traditionally, when the industry has a problem to solve, it can solve it either in-house with internal resources, or it can engage a third party service provider. These third party service providers can be consultants or contractors who are experts in the specific fields (Figure 1.4).

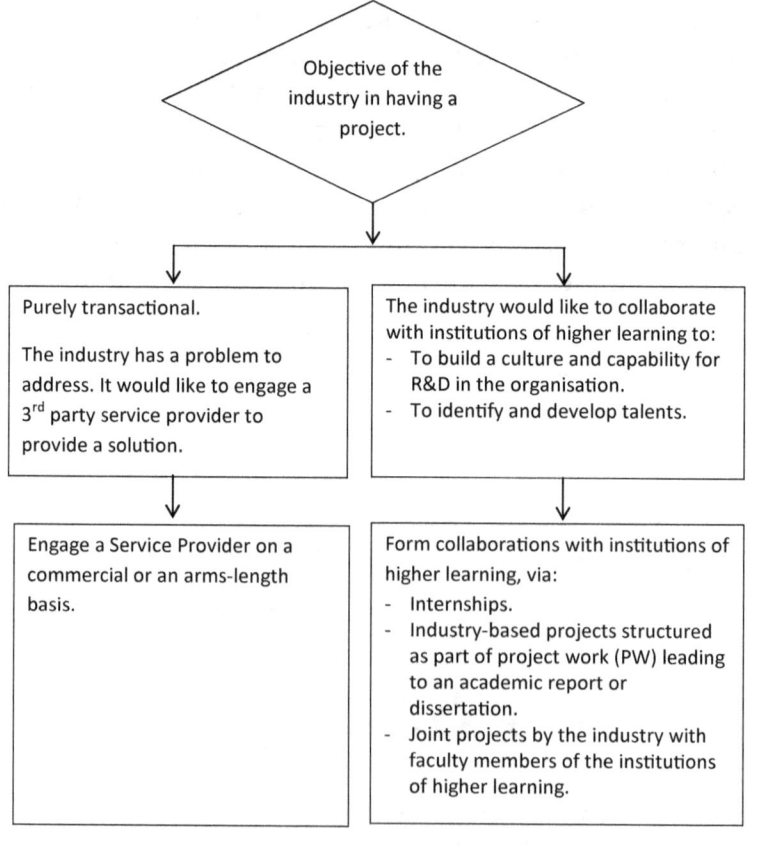

Figure 1.4   Objectives of the industry.

Increasingly, institutions of higher learning are also keen to provide an authentic learning experience for students. The mechanisms that they can leverage upon to achieve this include:

— Providing internship opportunities to students; or
— Structuring PW that can be done as part of the curriculum leading to an FYP report or dissertation.

Organizations can consider the latter approach if in addition to addressing a problem in practice, they would also like to build a culture and capability for research and development (R&D) in the organization. Furthermore, by collaborating with institutions of higher learning to provide industry-linked projects for students to work on, organizations can also take the opportunity of working with the students to identify potential talents for potential hiring in the future. By the same token, students should be incentivized to take their PW seriously as it may open doors for potential future career opportunities.

1.6. Can a lecturer who is not a domain expert of the project topic perform the role of the academic supervisor for the project effectively?

PW is directed at achieving the two objectives of developing process skills as well as enhancing substantive knowledge of a specific subject matter.

It will be ideal if the academic supervisor is an expert in both aspects so that a balanced approach can be taken. However, sometimes this is not possible. An academic supervisor who has worked for many years as a researcher in an academic institution may be well versed with the process of academic inquiry but may not be updated with the latest practices in the industry. On the other hand, an academic supervisor whose background was a practitioner from the industry may be very familiar with the practical aspects of the subject, but may not be so well versed with the process of academic inquiry or research skills.

Indeed, it is hoped that this book will help bridge this gap so that academic supervisors from different backgrounds can share a consistent approach towards designing and supervising PWs, and that students can better leverage on such supervision to enhance their learning (Figure 1.5).

In the case of industry-linked projects, the industry supervisor can make an important contribution to augment the input on the specific subject matter of the project.

1.7 What should be the appropriate duration of PW?

The duration of PW varies across different educational institutions. Typically, students may be given a year or a semester to

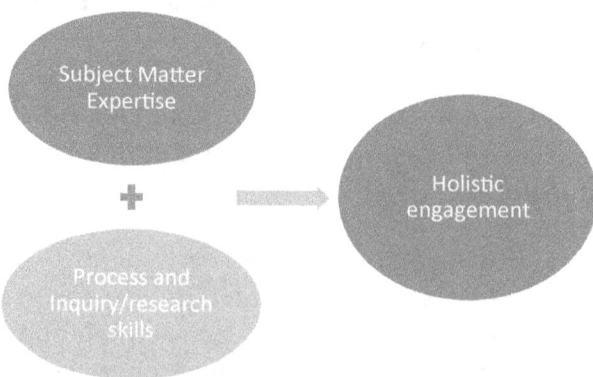

Figure 1.5 Skills required for successful collaboration and engagement between supervisor and candidate.

complete the project. However, it must be noted that these durations are just elapsed time. More importantly, the actual intended curriculum time for PW must be explicitly expressed in the design of the PW (Table 1.1).

For example, if a typical taught module entails 60 h of curriculum time (e.g., 4 h per week × 15 weeks in a semester), and the PW is intended to have the same academic weight as a typical taught module, then the PW should be designed to be completed within this amount of time, regardless of whether it is spread over a semester, a year or any other duration.

This is an important issue for the curriculum development and academic supervisory teams to consider. Very often, the actual time spent, and the expectations in terms of depth and quality of the deliverable of PW become inadvertently higher than what it should be. This may become overly burdensome to the students. The situation is aggravated when different students or groups of students are assigned different PWs where the time commitments required differ a lot.

Table 1.1 Duration for the completion of a project.

Level	Duration allowed for the completion of a project
Doctoral	2–4 years of candidature
Masters by research	1–2 years of candidature
Masters by coursework	One academic year or two semesters, to be done alongside four or five other modules of similar weight
Bachelor degree	One academic year or two semesters, to be done alongside four or five other modules of similar weight
Diploma	One to two semesters, to be done alongside about four other modules of similar weight in each semester

The rapid progress made in internet technology is also having a significant impact on the way PWs are designed and conducted. For example, in the past, a doctoral candidature would require four or more years of full-time research. This was not unreasonable as much time would need to be spent in physically ploughing through catalogues in the libraries, making photocopies of the journal articles, cutting and compiling newspaper cuttings, manually plotting graphs, etc.

Nowadays, with the advent of electronic database and citation management software, it is possible to complete a doctoral thesis without the need to even step into a physical library even once. The time needed to search and compile articles for literature review and the collation of secondary data is therefore reduced significantly. Likewise, software for word processing, data compilation and analyses have also made the preparation of the PW reports a lot more time efficient. Accordingly, considerably more meaningful and impactful deliverables can be accomplished within the project timeframe.

1.8 Is PW just another assignment given to students?

PW should not be just another assignment set by the academic staff to students at least for two reasons.

Firstly, the PW is directed at achieving the two objectives of process skills as well as substantive knowledge of a specific subject matter. Therefore, in terms of the integrative nature of PW (i.e. across the entire course of study be it in a Polytechnic Diploma or a University degree) as well as its academic weight (i.e. size), it should be differentiated from an ordinary assignment which is normally for partial fulfillment of a particular module.

Secondly, research and engagement with the industry is becoming a key component of the work of tertiary education institutions. It is therefore possible for PW to be done in conjunction with commissioned or consultancy projects with the industry. Such commissioned projects are likely to be spearheaded by faculty members who may include students to undertake part of the work with their PW. Once again, it must be emphasized that the nature of the students' involvement should be appropriate for their fulfillment of the curricular requirement of the PW, such as in data collection and analysis.

1.9 Must all PWs be about research? Must they be industry-linked?

Very often, PW carries some connotations that they must involve research. Indeed, there have been frequent questions from students as well as academic supervisors such as the following:

a. What constitutes a research project?

b. What are the differences between primary research, action research, applied research and consultancy projects?

c. What is the difference between an industry-linked project and a pure research project?

d. Must projects necessarily involve the use of sophisticated statistics? What are the differences between studies in natural and social sciences?

e. What is the role of an academic supervisor and a work supervisor?

f. Can someone who has little subject matter expertise of the project play the role of the academic supervisor for the project?

Confusion regarding the above question is frequently heard. Indeed, there can be many types of PWs, and it is important to categorize them. Why? Because, once you have categorized them appropriately, you will then be able to design the approach, and use the most suitable methodology.

It is also important to categorize them appropriately to ensure there is no misunderstanding between the expectations of the academic supervisor and the industry collaborator for those industry-linked projects. In continuation from there, the academic supervisory team may also want to consider if they need different rubrics to access the different types of projects.

The following matrix presents one way of categorizing the different types of projects, where they are distinguished by three dimensions described below (Table 1.2). The point to reiterate is that the project designer (i.e. either from the institution, or the industry, or jointly) must be cognizant of how

Table 1.2 Nature of the projects.

Context	Orientation	Methodology	Type Code
Institution–based (1)	Research-centric (1)	Qualitative (1)	1-1-1
		Quantitative (2)	1-1-2
		Mixed method (3)	1-1-3
	Practice-centric (2)	Qualitative (1)	1-2-1
		Quantitative (2)	1-2-2
		Mixed method (3)	1-2-3
Industry-linked (2)	Research-centric (1)	Qualitative (1)	2-1-1
		Quantitative (2)	2-1-2
		Mixed method (3)	2-1-3
	Practice-centric (2)	Qualitative (1)	2-2-1
		Quantitative (2)	2-2-2
		Mixed method (3)	2-2-3

the project is intended to be approached so that the appropriate guidance can be given to the students accordingly.

a. Context, i.e. whether they are institution-based (i.e. where the project is designed by the academic supervisor and not for submission to an external organization or client) or industry-based;

b. Orientation, i.e. whether they are research or practice-centric; and

c. Methodology, i.e. whether they employ qualitative, quantitative or mixed methods.

Please refer to Sections 3.12–3.14 for further discussions on qualitative, quantitative and mixed methods.

1.10 What are the differences between research-based and practice-based projects?

PWs can either be research-based or practice-based. Research-based PWs are more academic in nature. In most instances, they are dealing with primary research involving the collection of primary data. In the realm of science and technology, this type of PW may seek to examine a certain physical phenomenon by way of testing and analyzing the results derived from a set of experiments conducted in laboratories. In social science PWs, they may involve surveys to acquire data for analysis and drawing of inferences to certain social phenomenon. Sometimes, instead of seeking to collect primary data, research-centric projects may also involve the compilation of data from secondary sources in published articles in journals and other reports.

When in doubt, ask this question: "Does the project discover and contribute towards building new generic knowledge that was not previously known?" If the answer to this question is 'Yes', then this is likely to be a research-centric project.

On the other hand, practice-based PWs seek to solve problems in practice rather than discovering new knowledge. A few examples are shown in Table 1.3. You will note that in these examples, the projects may not involve the hypothesizing of new theories or lead to the discovery of new knowledge. They

Table 1.3 Practice-based projects.

Main objective of project	Subject domain/knowledge or skills required
Market research	a. Likely to be courses in the realm of business and management. b. Skills required include those for developing questionnaires, conducting surveys and statistical analysis of the survey results as well as relating these to the theories and concepts in business and management.
Constructing a wheelchair that can be used in off-road conditions	a. Likely to be in engineering courses. b. It is likely that such projects will entail at least the aspects of engineering design, as well as fabrication. In the former, the use of computer aided design should be included. c. A further possible inclusion is the aspect of a financial feasibility study. The latter aspect can be done in conjunction with the business school.
Developing a website for a company, or developing a mobile app for a certain purpose	a. Possible courses that can have projects like this include those in IT, multimedia or business. b. For those in IT and multimedia, obviously the emphasis will be on the effective use of the programming knowledge and technology that is covered in the course of study. For business courses, the emphasis of such projects will likely focus on creativity and effectiveness from the perspective of corporate and marketing communications.

may just be applied research where existing theories or knowledge covered in the course of study are applied to solve some practical real world problems.

1.11 Are research-based PWs more prestigious than practice-based PWs?

It all depends. If a PW is set out to achieve a research objective, then it should be done as a research project, and vice-versa. It is therefore not necessary to debate if one type of PW is more prestigious than the other.

But, how does this question arise? The notion of research is generally associated with work done in universities, whereas work done in polytechnics and vocational institutions is more practice-oriented. While this is true, practice-based projects are also conducted routinely in universities, especially in Master of Business Administration (MBA), architecture, engineering and design programmes, including those listed in Table 1.3 earlier.

While research projects seek to discover new knowledge, practice-based projects seek to solve a problem in practice. In both instances, problem-solving skills are employed to deal with the issues at hand. These problem-solving skills are known as the 'methodology' in the context of PWs. Please see Sections 2.9–2.15.

In conclusion, it is essential to recognize that there are different types of projects requiring different skillsets. It is not necessary to dwell on the debate of which is more prestigious or more difficult. What is more important is to ensure that there is a good fit between the supervisors and the student with respect to the nature of the project. This is to ensure that the student will receive the appropriate guidance and that they will not be penalized for potential mismatch in expectations.

1.12 Must practice-based PWs be done in collaboration with the industry?

Both research-centric and practice-centric PWs can be done in collaboration with an industry partner or supervised entirely within the purview of the academic institution. If it is done with an industry partner, it is likely that the academic staff will need to have prior discussions and consensus on how to frame the PW so that deliverables are feasible within the framework of PWs.

In industry-linked projects, some funding may be provided by the industry partner. An agreement or a Memorandum of Understanding (MOU) may be signed for this purpose.

1.13 What is Design Thinking?

In recent years, there has been a surge of interest in design thinking. Some have even suggested that Design Thinking is superior to the traditional methodical research and problem-solving protocols, which entail the key components of literature review or situation analysis, data collection and analysis, as well as discussions of the results and formulation of recommendations. These kinds of comparison may be confusing to some.

Are they really different? Do these ideas have to be mutually exclusive or do they reinforce one another instead?

Herbert A. Simon is regarded as the founding father of several of today's important scientific domains, including artificial intelligence, information processing, complex systems, and computer simulation of scientific discovery. In his 1969 book, '*The Sciences of the Artificial*', he devised a three stage process for rational decision making involving intelligence gathering, design, and making choices (Simon, 1969; cited in Forbes, 2014). In Figure 1.6, it will be intuitive to see that these activities are indeed not so different from familiar approach to research and problemsolving, involving data collection and/or literature review, choosing the methodology, analyzing the results, making sense of the findings, and eventually, synthesizing the solutions so as to make the findings useful for application in the real world or contribution to knowledge.

Later, in the 1980s, the work of Rolf Feste of Stanford University gained momentum, which saw the popularization of the concept of design thinking as a method of creative action. Essentially, design thinking can be understood as 'a formal method for practical, creative resolution of problems or issues, with the

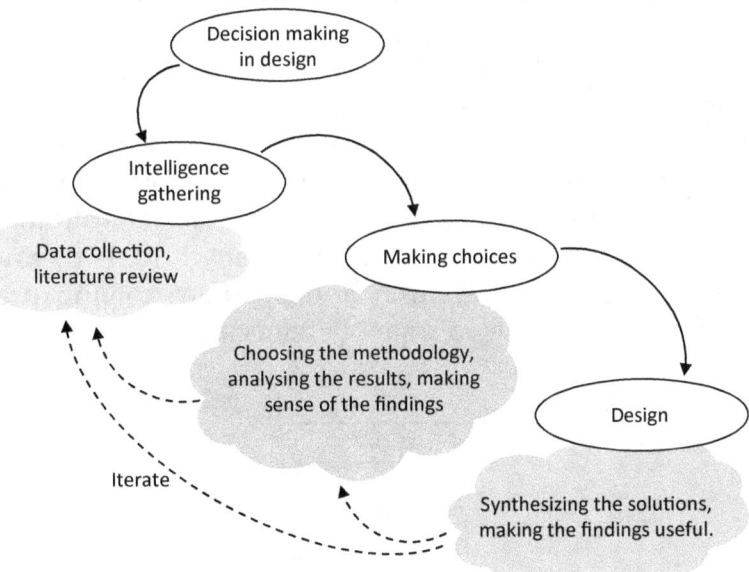

Figure 1.6 Intelligence, Design, Choice (IDC) process for rational decision making.
Source: Adapted from Herbert Simon (1969).

intent of an improved future result.' In other words, through designing, the perceptions, thoughts and ideas are actualized.

Forbes (2014) also discussed another framework for design thinking which entails the activities of empathize, define, ideate, prototype, test.

So, how do these contemporary design thinking concepts relate to the traditional research and problem-solving protocols?

In any design process, the starting point is to understand the needs and empathize with the problem to be solved. Is this not similar to 'intelligence gathering' in Figure 1.6 or the endeavor of building a literature review or situation analysis in the traditional research and problem-solving protocol?

The next stage of the IDC process is 'design' which entails 'analyze'. But, in order to analyze, do you not require the collection of relevant data? Would this not in effect be data collection and analysis? Figure 1.7 mentioned the stages of prototyping and testing. Are these concepts not similar to hypothesis postulations and testings? Based on the analyses, you can synthesize to explore the realm of possibilities, construct solutions and make choices for application in the real world. Is this not the same in traditional research and problem-solving protocol during which you also make observations from the data

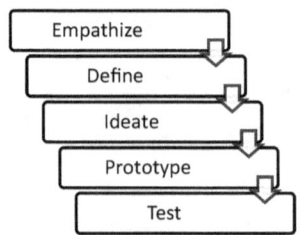

Figure 1.7   Stages of design thinking.

Source: Forbes (2014)

Curricular Objectives of 'Project Work'   21

Research and problem solving protocols	Corresponding concepts of Design Thinking
Literature review, situation analysis.	Intelligence gathering, problem definition.
Data collection and analysis.	Prototyping, testing, analysis
Discussion of results, formulation of recommendations.	Analysis, synthesis

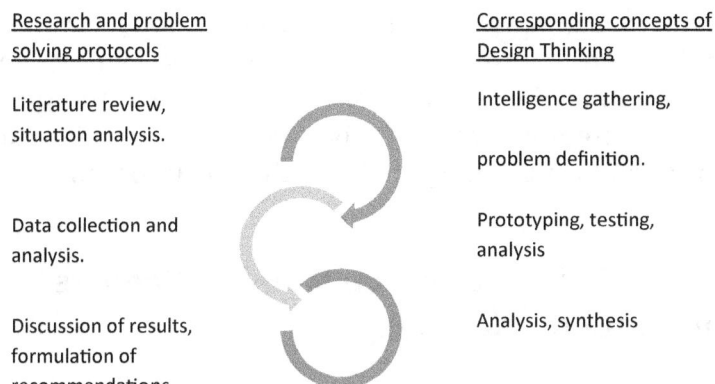

Figure 1.8 Reinforcing concepts of design thinking with research and problem-solving protocols

analysis, identify options, discuss alternatives and finally make recommendations?

Perhaps, what really matters is that the traditional research and problem-solving protocols would normally be directed at establishing relationships amongst 'factors', using such methodologies as hypothesis testing, correlation analysis, scenario planning, etc., whereas the notions of design thinking (Figure 1.8) will be more proximate to the practiced-based type of projects which are more applied in nature. In this kind of project, what comes immediately to the minds of many people will be the design of a new product or a gadget, a building, a township, which are tangible. However, beyond physical products, problem solving in the real world would also entail soft system solutions, such as a business strategy, a public policy, a civic and community programme, etc. While this is not within the realm of the mainstream design and creative community, the principles of design thinking should still be applicable.

Thus, with this brief debate about design thinking, we would like to suggest that design thinking is not exclusive from the traditional research and problem-solving protocol. Conversely, design thinking is a mental attitude which we can embrace in research and problem solving to further unleash the power of analysis and creativity of the individual in the pursuit of knowledge and solution building to make the world better.

1.14 Must PWs lead to publication of papers in academic journals?

An academic journal is a periodical whereby scholarly articles are published. The better ones are internationally peer reviewed whereby papers intended to be published are vetted by a review panel typically consisting of fellow academics who are experienced and regarded as experts in the subject matter.

Publishing in academic journals is therefore a central aspect of research, particularly at the university level. However, for students, this is encouraged but need not be compulsory. Where publication in academic journals is pursued, it is usually done in conjunction with the academic supervisor(s) for the PW. If the students have made substantive contribution to the research, they may be included as co-authors. Otherwise, they can be included in the acknowledgement.

Polytechnics are also doing more and more research. Likewise, it is encouraged but not necessary for PW to work towards having the outcome published in an academic journal.

Due to the nature of academic journals, PWs that are pursued with the intention of having the outcome submitted for publication in academic journals will likely be designed as research-centric from the onset. Conversely, PWs that are practice-centric may not lend themselves suitable for publication in academic journals especially if this arose as an after-thought.

Another point to note is that academic journals are ranked competitively according to their impact factor. The higher a journal is ranked, the more selective it will be in accepting papers for publication. Thus, it is perfectly fine for less experienced academics and early researchers to select the journals for submission for potential publication with realistic consideration of the ranking of the journal and the nature of the paper.

Finally, whether the PW is eventually submitted for publication in an academic journal or not, this should not be part of the academic deliverable of the PW. For related topic, please refer to Section 2.2.

1.15 How to write a project proposal?

A project proposal is a document that spells out the specification, definition or what the project entails.

There are various types of project proposals. For example,

a. Project proposals put up by the academic supervisors to invite students to sign up for the projects as required in the curriculum.

b. Project proposals submitted by students. Some institutions or programmes of studies will require students to consider and submit their own project proposals to be evaluated by the institution.

c. Project proposal put up by the faculty staff to potential industry collaborators to seek collaboration or sponsorship.

The details and length of each of them will be different. Naturally, for higher levels of studies such as at the doctoral level, the project proposal will be in the form of a research proposal. This can be a substantive academic paper itself encompassing literature reviews and detailed discussions of the methodology. For the purpose of the discussions here, the focus will be on the context of (a) and (b) whereby the project will form only one of the many modules or components of a programme of studies. For example, this may be the final year project of an undergraduate degree programme or a polytechnic diploma programme, PW in the 'A' level curriculum, or an Extended Essay in the IB programme.

Regardless, project proposals should include the following primary components necessary to describe the project:

a. Title of the project. Keep this short and simple.

b. State objectives of the project. Again, keep this short, simple, and directly to the point. Elaborations on the rationale and other details can be done at the background section.

c. State if the project is industry linked or commissioned by a company or an organization. If it is, state the name of the company or organization that commissioned the project.

d. State if the project is research-centric or practice-centric. Please refer to Section 1.10 earlier for detailed discussion on this matter. This is important as it will have direct implications on the methodology. Flowing from this, this will also be an important consideration for the matching of students with the appropriate interest or skills for the project.

e. Background — This is for discussing the motivation or the need for the project. For example, this may be due to an identified gap in knowledge of the subject matter, or a problem in practice that needs to be solved. Preferably, the research questions, hypothesis, or conceptual framework of inquiry should be stated here, even though these may change when the research gets underway.

f. Methodology — This description in this section may start with explaining if the primary methodology to be used will be quantitative or qualitative. Beyond that, it will be necessary to elaborate with some details such as hypothesis testing or correlation analysis will be employed. If it involves surveys, the approach to do sampling will also be needed. Please refer to Section 4.1 also.

g. Key sources for literature review — Please list a preliminary list of key references, say three to five for a project report of about 4000 words.

In addition, it will also be very helpful to identify and highlight which modules or topics of the programme of studies the project will relate to.

h. Personnel of the project — This will include at least the names and relevant information of the key personnel as shown in Table 1.4.

i. In the case of project proposals submitted by students for evaluation, it is also useful for some other relevant information to be included, such as a brief description by the students to indicate their suitability for the project, usually due to the interest or special skills they may have.

j. Project Schedule — This may be in the form of a Gantt chart as shown in Annex B. At the project proposal stage, the level of details required may not be so extensive. Nevertheless, they should at least indicate the key milestones such as for the following:

— Project start date,

— Completion of the literature review section,

Table 1.4 Key personal of a project.

Parties in the project	Remarks
Academic supervisor	Where this is a project offered by the academic supervisor for selection by the students.
Industry supervisor	Where it is an industry-linked project.
Students	Where it is a project proposal submitted by the student(s).

- Completion of the methodology section,
- The start and finishing date for data collection,
- The submission of the completed draft report, and
- The submission of the final report.
- Project end date.

k. Budget — A budget will need to be provided, especially where internal or external funding is required. A budget may be required for the purchase of equipment, software, or for expenses to conduct surveys or other ways of collecting data. A breakdown of the individual cost items will be necessary.

Ethics declaration may be structured as part of the project proposal or attached as an Annex. In some other institutions, an ethics declaration is submitted separately after the project is accepted at the face value. Please see Chapter 6 also.

As can be seen from the above, project proposals entail a fair bit of thinking and planning prior to the commencement of the project. It is important that sufficient time should be set aside to allow this process to be undertaken with care and not to be rushed. Please see Annex B for a sample project proposal, as well as Section 5.3 and Annex C about project schedule.

A project proposal that is done well will go a long way to ensure the success of the project. Indeed, doing the project proposal properly will help to identify potential risks and allow these to be mitigated in the project plan. When writing the project proposals, such as in stating the objectives, research questions or developing the methodology, one has to be realistic about what can be accomplished within the time frame and the resource availability, knowledge and skills of the students. The identification of the key sources of information will help to ensure that the project proposed is non-trivial and is suitable for an academic discourse. The pre-planning of the methodology will help to ensure that it is feasible. Furthermore, it will also help identify the budget needed.

On the other hand, a project proposal that is rushed, or devoid of essential details may see various difficulties when the project starts. Some of the avoidable but common issues encountered by students include:

— Difficulties in identifying relevant sources during literature review.

— Complications in doing data collection due to scheduling problems or difficulties in getting samples.

— Problems in performing analysis due to incomplete data.

— Event cancelled in a project that is centred on organizing the event for the client, etc.

CHAPTER 2

STRUCTURE OF THE REPORT/ DISSERTATION/THESIS

After reading this chapter, you will be able to:

— *Determine the structure of the report.*

— *Understand what contents should be included in each chapter.*

— *Choose the methodology for the project.*

— *Write citations and references.*

2.1 What is the structure of PW report, which may also be known as a dissertation or a thesis?

While care must be taken not to overly prescribe a fixed and rigid structure for a project work (PW) report, it is also important to note that the debate on this issue should not be about the choice or preference of the supervisors or the students. A key consideration is that it should be consistent with the over-arching approach for research and problem-solving inquiry.

The PW report should be presented with an organized and logical structure. This is not just for aesthetic reasons. This in fact is a leading indicator that reflects the state of mind of the students, whether they have given sufficient thought to organize and present an involved set of information. Otherwise, the report may just become a haphazard and incoherent compilation of unprocessed data on which relationships are only weakly established or non-apparent at all.

Accordingly, a typical structure of such a document should reflect the process inquiry and may comprise the following key chapters or sections:

a. Introduction

b. Literature review

c. Methodology

d. Analysis

e. Conclusions

While the structure of the PW reports may be organized in a certain manner, it does not mean that the thinking process must be restricted to follow this structure sequentially as in 'A' below. As working through projects is basically a creative process, it is likely to be iterative as shown in 'B' (Figure 2.1). For example, even if we have already completed the data collection and are working on discussing the results, there may still be a need to revisit the literature review in order to clarify a piece of information, review a point or fortify an argument.

Essays are generally prescribed as part of the deliverables for a module for formative purposes. The topic in an essay is relatively specific and the turnaround time given is usually short, say from a few days to a week or two. Generally, there is less emphasis on the collection of primary data for involved analysis. Rather, the emphasis will be on building an argument for a certain point of view. Accordingly, Students may find that the structure required for essays may be different from what is normally found in dissertations and thesis, as shown in Figure 2.2. Nonetheless, the basic premise of having an overall purpose within the context of a coherently constructed academic inquiry is similar.

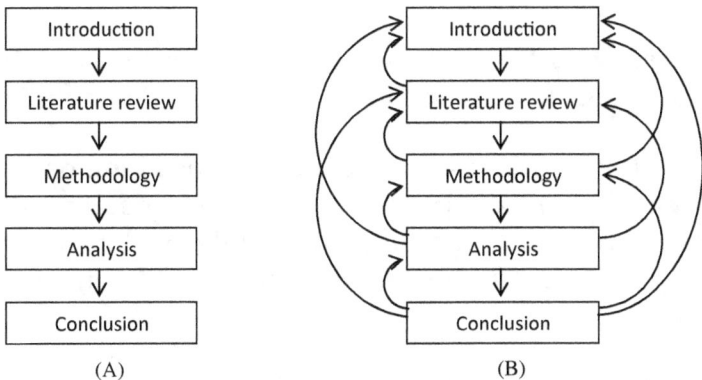

Figure 2.1 Iterative process in project-based learning.

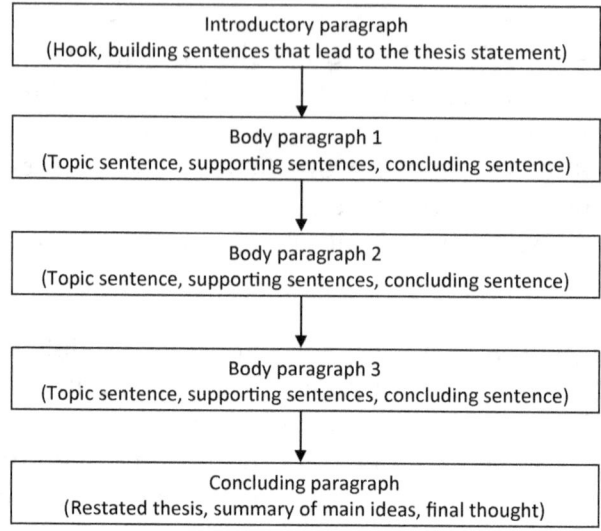

Figure 2.2   Structure of an essay.

2.2 What is a publishable paper?

A 'Publishable paper' is a formal piece of academic work written in the form that is suitable to be submitted for publication in a journal. A 'Publishable paper' could be an alternative deliverable for a PW curriculum.

In that case, why isn't the requirement of PW for a published paper to be submitted instead of a 'publishable paper'?

It is 'publishable' and not 'published' because for a paper to be acceptable for publishing by a journal, it will need to undergo peer review. It is likely that the papers will also be subjected to professional considerations beyond the level intended for the curriculum.

Furthermore, it will take a long time for a paper to be reviewed before it is accepted for publishing. It is not uncommon for a paper to take 6 months to a year from the submission of the first draft to its eventual publication, if at all.

Hence, for the purpose of fulfilling a curriculum requirement, a 'publishable' paper would suffice, if the objective of the curriculum is really intended to train the students for academic writing. Otherwise, a normal project report, thesis or dissertation will also suffice.

Notwithstanding, if the PW report is in the form of a dissertation, thesis or 'publishable paper, the generic framework of having chapters or sections for Introduction, Literature review, Methodology, Analysis/Discussion, and Conclusions should still serve as a useful reference.

2.3 How long should the PW deliverable be in terms of word count?

There is a range. It depends primarily on three factors:

a. The level of the course. Generally, the more senior the programmer is, the more substantive the deliverable required. For example, the requirements for a final year thesis for an undergraduate course should be higher than that for a diploma course.

b. The time given to complete the PW. Generally, the more the time given, the longer the deliverable required. In this regard, care should be taken to consider the actual budgeted time rather than the elapsed time. Please see Section 2.6.

c. The nature of the PW. Generally, reports for qualitative PW tend to have more words than those for quantitative PW. On the other hand, quantitative PW may include the tabulation of more data either in the main report or in the appendices.

Table 2.1 can be referred to as a guide:

Table 2.1 Number of words in the PW report.

Level of study	Number of words in the PW report
Doctoral	30,000–80,000
Masters	15,000–25,000
Bachelor degree	10,000–20,000
Diploma	3,000–5,000
Term paper	1,500–2,000

2.4 Are there conventions to follow in terms of formatting?

a. 'Publishable paper' vs Dissertation vs Thesis

There are a variety of ways to organize the format of PW reports. Some examples are summarized in Table 2.2:

As mentioned earlier, essays are generally prescribed as part of the deliverables for a module for formative purposes. The topic in an essay is relatively specific and the turnaround time given is usually short, say from a few days to a week or two. As such, there are usually only simple formatting guidelines which the instructor may prescribe.

At the other end of the continuum, the terms *dissertation* and *thesis* are primarily used in universities. In the United States, it is commonly held that a thesis is submitted at the end of one's master's degree, and dissertation is submitted at the end of a PhD. However, in the United Kingdom, it may be the other way round. In some other universities, these terms may be used interchangeably.

In terms of word processing formatting, most universities will require theses and dissertations to be formatted with the prescribed cover page, table of contents, list of tables, list of figures, numbered chapters and appendices. It is also

Table 2.2 Format of a PW report.

Type of PW report	Remarks
Essay	Minimal requirements for elaborate formatting. The instructor may prescribe their own guidelines.
Publishable paper	In adherence with the formatting convention of journals. Some examples are: American Psychological Association (APA) Style, which is commonly used in social sciences: http://www.apastyle.org/ Harvard referencing system, which is commonly used in science as well has humanities: http://www.deakin.edu.au/students/study-support/referencing/harvard Please see Section 2.6 for further discussions on citation and referencing styles.
Thesis or Dissertation	Usually include a cover page, table of contents, statement of acknowledgement, numbered chapters, and in some instances even numbered sections and paragraphs. They are also usually bound in the format of a book.

commonly acceptable for a statement of acknowledgement to be included.

Taking into consideration the educational objectives of PW to develop competencies for research and the associated academic and professional writing, an integrated approach for formatting as summarized in Table 2.3 later is recommended.

b. Numbering of paragraphs

Most mainstream styles for academic writing do not entail numbering of the paragraphs. On the other hand, the numbering of paragraphs is commonly found in executive papers and professional reports used in management.

---

[1] However, in some format guidelines, this may be included either as a footnote, or a special paragraph at the end of the paper.

Table 2.3 Numbering of paragraphs.

Level	Essays	Publishable paper	Thesis, Dissertation	Professional reports	Integrated approach
Cover page with institution's logo and particulars of candidate and his course of study, etc.	N.A.	N.A.	Yes.	Yes.	Yes.
Acknowledgement	N.A.	Not necessary.[1]	Yes.	Yes.	Yes.
Table of contents	N.A.	N.A.	Yes.	Yes.	Yes.
List of tables, figures, acronyms, etc.	N.A.	N.A.	Yes.	Yes.	Yes.
Abstract	N.A.	Yes.	Yes.	Yes.	Yes.
Numbered chapters and sub-sections in chapters	N.A.	N.A.	Yes.	Yes.	Yes.
Numbered paragraphs	N.A.	N.A.	N.A.	Yes.	N.A.
Citations and references	Optional.	Yes.	Yes.	Good to have.	Good to have.

The numbering of paragraphs can be very effective in helping the author form connections of the various paragraphs to ensure they flow well. Accordingly, even for formats that do not require or disallow numbering of paragraphs, students can still consider numbering the paragraphs in their initial drafts. They can remove the numbering later when they are satisfied that the overall structure and flow of the dissertation has taken a substantive and stable form.

c. Labeling of figures and tables

As general principle, figures and tables ought to be labeled. This is also the requirement of most formatting conventions.

Structure of The Report/Dissertation/Thesis

The next question is how should these be labelled. The following guidelines are recommended:

i. The labels of figures and tables should include their number and title.

ii. The labels of figures should be placed below the figures. On the other hand, the labels for tables should be placed on top of the tables.

iii. For PW reports, theses and dissertations that run into several chapters and numbered accordingly, a good practice is to number the figures and tables in accordance with the chapter numbering, for example,

- The first figure in Chapter 1 should be numbered as Figure 1.1.
- The second figure in Chapter 1 should be numbered as Figure 1.2.
- The first figure in Chapter 2 should be numbered as Figure 2.1.
- The second figure in Chapter 2 should be numbered as Figure 2.2.

    .... and so on.

- Likewise,
- The first table in Chapter 1 should be numbered as Table 1.1.
- The second table in Chapter 1 should be numbered as Table 1.2.
- The first table in Chapter 2 should be numbered as Table 2.1.
- The second table in Chapter 2 should be numbered as Table 2.2.

    .... and so on.

iv. On the other hand, essays and journal papers are generally not so long. Instead of chapters, the content may just be organized into different sections indicated by section headings that are not numbered. For these, the numbering of the figures and tables can be sequential from Figure 1 to the last or Table 1 to the last. For an essay, as presented above, there may not be any sections labeled.

Please refer to the way figures and tables are labeled in this book. They are based on the guidelines presented above.

2.5 What are the commonly used citations and referencing styles?

The APA style is adopted in many institutions. But, each institution may stipulate its own format. Regardless, the most important thing to note is consistency. As an alternative to APA format, other formats like the Harvard referencing system or those that are adopted by mainstream journals may also be used. These were also discussed in the earlier section.

There are three things to discuss, i.e.

a. the referencing format in the reference list or bibliography,

b. format for in-text citations,

c. format for dealing with multiple authors in in-text citations.

These are elaborated below.

a. The referencing format in the reference list or bibliography

A reference list and a bibliography are similar. They are both composed of entries of the full description of the cited materials displayed at the end of the PW report. These entries are arranged alphabetically in accordance with the names of the authors.

All materials that are cited in text must be included in the reference list or the bibliography. For the bibliography, it may also include other works that the author consulted, but not cited in the text.

Some basic guidelines for format citations and references are summarized below.

General notes:

— The format structure is the 'author-date-title-publisher' citation system. This is also the approach adopted in both the APA style and the Harvard system.

— Use 'sentence case' for the title, i.e., capitalize only the first letter of the title and not every word of it.

— The title of books, including any subtitles, should be italicized.

— If no author is provided, use the article title as the key identifier of the reference.

— If no publication date is provided, just indicate it as not dated in this format: (n.d.).

— If the volume or issue number cannot be located, simply do not include it in the citation.

— For newspaper and magazines, it is important to indicate the city where they are published. This is because it is not uncommon for newspaper and/or magazines with similar titles in different cities.

— The references should be listed with 'hanging indent' in the reference list or the bibliography.

Specific notes for online resources:

— Generally, this will be the same as that for print resources, except that the URL should be provided. Alternatively, the digital object identifier (DOI) can be provided. The DOI is an assigned number that helps link content to its location on the Internet.

— Generally, it is not a requirement to include the date of access for online sources, although this practice is also quite common.

— Some URLs may need to run into multiple lines. In this situation, the URL can be 'broken' into subsequent lines before punctuations (except for http://). Alternatively, it is also acceptable to just provide the home page of the website concerned without the extensions that provides the linkage directly to the article concerned. The home page of the website will usually contain a search function for readers to search with the specific author or article title to access the article eventually.

Examples of listings of references in the reference list or bibliography are provided below:

i. A journal article in print

   Format: Author, A.A. (Publication Year). Article title. Periodical Title, Volume (Issue), pp. xx–xx.

   Example:
   Ho, M.W., Ho, K.H.D. (2006). Risk management in large physical infrastructure investments: The context of seaport infrastructure development and Investment. *Journal of Maritime Economics & Logistics*, 6(2), pp. 140–168.

ii. A journal article found online

   Format: Author, A.A. (Publication Year). Article title. Periodical Title, Volume (Issue), pp. xx–xx. DOI: XX. XXXXX or Retrieved from journal URL

Example:
Ho, M.W. & Ho, K.H.D. (2006). Risk management in large physical infrastructure investments: The context of seaport infrastructure development and Investment. *Journal of Maritime Economics & Logistics*, 6(2), pp. 140–168. DOI: http://dx.doi.org/10.1057/palgrave.mel.9100153

iii. A book

Format: Author, A.A. (Year of Publication). Title of work. Publisher City, State: Publisher.

Example:
Baron, D. (2000). *Business and its environment*, 3rd Edition Upper Saddle River, NJ: Prentice Hall.

iv. An e-book (electronic book)

Format: Author, A.A. (Year of Publication). Title of work [E-Reader Version]. Publisher. Retrieved from http://xxxx or DOI:xxxx

Example:
Speed, H. (2004). *The practice and science of drawing*. Retrieved from http://www.gutenberg.org/files/ 14264/14264-h/14264-h.htm

v. A book found in a database

Format: Author, A.A. (Year of Publication). Title of work. Retrieved from http://xxxx or DOI: xxxx

Example:
Sayre, Rebecca K., Devercelli, A.E., Neuman, M.J., & Wodon, Q. (2015). *Investment in early childhood development: Review of The World Bank's recent experience*. DOI: 10.1596/978-1-4648-0403-8

vi. A chapter in an edited book

Format: Author, A. A., & Author, B. B. (Year of publication). Title of chapter. In A. A. Editor & B. B. Editor (Eds.), Title of book (pages of chapter). Location: Publisher.

Example:
Krajcik, J. S., & Blumenfeld, P. C. (2006). Project-based learning.

In R. Keith Sawyer (Ed.), *The Cambridge Handbook of the Learning Sciences* (pp. 317–334). Cambridge: Cambridge University Press.

vii. A magazine article in print with the author indicated

Format: Author, A.A. (Year, month of Publication). Article title. Magazine Title, Volume (Issue), pp. xx–xx.

Example:
Ryan, J. (2015). SAF50: The RSN through the years. NAVY, Republic of Singapore Navy, (01), pp. 10–15.

viii. A magazine article found online

Format: Author, A.A. (Year, Month of Publication). Article title. Magazine Title, Volume (Issue), Retrieved from http://xxxx

Example:
Langgley, L. (2017, Feb). Whales with Caribbean accents and other animals' dialects. *National Geographic*. Retrieved from http://news.nationalgeographic.com

ix. A newspaper article in print with author indicated

Format: Author, A.A. (Year, Month Date of Publication). Article title. Newspaper Title, pp. xx–xx.

Example:
Goh, E Y. (2016, Feb 29). The bane of negative interest rates. *The Straits Times*, Singapore, p. C3.

x. A newspaper article found online with author indicated

Format: Author, A.A. (Year, Month Date of Publication). Article title. Newspaper Title. Retrieved from newspaper homepage URL

Example:
Lim, A. (2016, Feb 29). Parliament: Cross Island Line to have about 30 stations, with 600,000 trips made daily: Khaw Boon Wan. *The Straits Times*, Singapore. Retrieved from http://www.straitstimes.com/Singapore

xi. A website article with an author

Format: Author, A.A. (Year, Month Date of Publication). Article title. Retrieved from URL.

Example:
Whittell, I. (2016, Feb 29). Wenger challenges Arsenal to rebound from setback at Old Trafford. *AFP News*. Retrieved from https://sg.sports.yahoo.com/news/wenger-challenges-arsenal-rebound-setback-old-trafford-022347748--sow.html

xii. A website article without an author

Format: Article title. (Year, Month Date of Publication or assessed). Retrieved from URL

Example:
New rules on pros fighting at Olympics set for vote. (2016, March 1). Retrieved from https://sg.sports.yahoo.com/news/rules-pros-fighting-olympics-set-vote-165213818--spt.html

xiii. A reference where the author is an organization:

In this case, mention the organization's name in full. If the organization has a well-known abbreviation, include the abbreviation in brackets.

Example:
Economic Development Board [EDB]. (2015). Annual Report 2015 of the Singapore Economic Development Board. Retrieved from www.edb.gov.sg.

b. Format for in-text citations

As the name suggests, in-text citations are the mention of the materials cited within the text of the PW report. There are three approaches to, include in-text citations. Please see the examples below:

Approach A – as part of the signal phrase and flows as part of a sentence in the text, example:

According to Yogaraj (1998), APA style is a difficult citation format for first-time learners.

Approach B – parenthesis format, i.e. usually placed at the end of a sentence, example:

APA style is a difficult citation format for first-time learners (Yogaraj, 1998).

Approach C – as a quotation, example:

According to Yogaraj (1998), "Students often had difficulty using APA style, especially when it was their first time".

Reminder: For every source that is cited in text, the full description of the source must be given in the reference list or the bibliography at the end of the PW report.

c. Format for dealing with multiple authors in in-text citations

In the three examples given in Section 2.4.2b, only one author was involved. How should we format these when there is more than one author? Please see the guidelines below.

i. A reference by two authors

Name both authors each time you cite the work. Use the word "and" between the authors' names within the text and use the ampersand in the parentheses.

Example:
Research by Wegener and Petty (1994) supports the notion that ...

(Wegener & Petty, 1994).

ii. A reference by three to five authors

List all the authors in the signal phrase or in parentheses the first time you cite the source. Use the word "and" between the authors' names within the text and use the ampersand in the parentheses.

Example:
Yogaraj, Amos, Andrew, Berry, and Harlow (1998) argued that ...

... (Yogaraj, Amos, Andrew, Berry, & Harlow, 1998).

In subsequent citations of the same reference, show only the name of the first author followed by "*et al.*" The word "*et al.*" came from the Latin word '*et alia*'. It means "... among others".

Example:
Yogaraj *et al.* (1998) disagreed with the view that ...

... (Yogaraj *et al.*, 1998).

iii. **A reference by six or more authors**

Since the list is rather long, we may use the first author's name followed by *et al.* from the first instance the reference is mentioned.

Example:
Brooke *et al.* (2002) suggested that ....

(Brooke *et al.*, 2002).

iv. **A reference where the author is not mentioned:**

In this instance, the reference may be cited by its title or the first word or phrase of the title, but the titles should be put within quotation marks.

Example, for the earlier example shown in Section 2.4.2(a)(xii) earlier:
"New rules" (2016) proposed that ...

... ("New rules", 2016).

v. **A reference where the author is listed as "Anonymous":**

In this case, simply use the name Anonymous as the author in the reference list, bibliography and correspondingly, in the in-text citations.

Example:
Research by Anonymous (2015) supports the notion that ...

... (Anonymous, 2015).

vi. **A source where the author is an organization**

For the first time-the source is cited, provide the full name of the organization with the abbreviation if this is available.

Example:
The Singapore Economic Development Board [EDB] (2015) describes ...

... (The Singapore Economic Development Board [EDB], 2015).

In the subsequent citation of the same reference, we can use the abbreviation only.

The EDB (2015) describes ...

... (EDB, 2015).

If an abbreviation is not available, or if the abbreviation is not commonly known or if full name is not too lengthy, we may just use the full name.

Example:
Netball Singapore (2011) highlights that ...

... (Netball Singapore, 2011).

vii. Where two or more sources are cited for the same idea

In this case, simply include the sources, order them the same way they appear in the reference list or bibliography (i.e., alphabetically), and separate them with semi-colons.

Example:
Hui (2002) and Tracy (1983) analyzed that ...

... (Hui, 2002; Tracy, 1983).

viii. Where the authors have the same family name

In order to avoid confusion, the initials can also be included to describe authors' names so as to distinguish them.

Example:
W. Ho (1996) and D. Ho (2012) researched on ...

... (W. Ho, 1996; D. Ho, 2012).

ix. Where two or more sources are by the same author in the same year

In this case, we can use the lower-case alphabets to distinguish them in the reference list or bibliography as well as in the in-text citation.

Example:
Research by David (1999a) illustrated that ...

David (1999b) added that ...

x. Citing secondary sources

As a guide, attempt should be made to locate the original source and cite it directly. Where this is not possible, we can follow the example given below. But, we must not forget to list the secondary source in the reference list or bibliography.

Example:
Lee (as cited in Josephine, 2003) argued that ...

2.6 What is an Abstract? Is an Abstract the same as a Synopsis?

An abstract can be considered as a brief summary of a dissertation. It should mention briefly the motivation leading to the study, the methodology employed and the key findings and recommendations.

It is not uncommon to read abstracts that do not mention the key findings and seem more like a repeat of the introduction. These will not be good abstracts.

For the purpose discussed in this book, it can be taken that Abstract and Synopsis refer to the same thing.

2.7 What should be included in the Introduction?

The introduction chapter should give the brief background of the project, for example, the motivation for doing the project, why and how it came about. If the project arose out of a collaboration with an external or industry client, this should also be stated.

The introduction chapter should state explicitly the objectives of the project. This is a very important matter. At the end of the project, students should check that the conclusions do address the objectives as stated in the introduction chapter.

2.8 What should be included in the literature review?

You may read this in conjunction with Section 4.7 regarding effective academic writing.

The objective of the literature review is to establish what is already known or what has already been done previously, i.e., before we embark on the project. This is to ensure that we are building upon what has been done previously rather than repeating what is already known.

To work on the literature review, you can try to ask and answer the following questions:

a. What is the existing body of knowledge regarding the subject matter?

b. What papers have been published, by whom, and what were the key findings?

Another intention of the literature review is to encourage students to read widely on the subject matter of the project they are working on. As discussed in Figure 1.1 earlier, being familiar with the subject matter of the project is one of the twin objectives of PW. The other objective of PW is to develop the skills for problem solving and research.

What are the common challenges faced by students with regard to literature review?

Not surprisingly, many students at this stage of their education are relatively inexperienced with research or project work. The common pitfalls that we have observed include:

a. Students were just narrating what they have read without including any of their original writing arising from their critical thinking on what they have read or observed.

b. The paragraphs do not flow from one to the other. They are incoherent.

c. Students just wrote from their feelings, personal opinions or hearsay without referencing or citations.

d. Students just cut and paste from sources from the internet, save for some editing to prevent them from being picked up by Turnitin for plagiarism. As a result, the sentences and paragraphs may become even more disconnected and incoherent.

e. Students may have come across some paragraphs or diagrams that they find very impressive. They just included them in the report even though they may not be relevant nor understand them.

How to overcome the above challenges? For a start, students need to learn and develop the confidence to read critically by asking and probing the following questions:

a. Where are the knowledge gaps still existing?

b. Were there limitations in the previous work done, such as whether sampling was too narrow or inappropriate, or if there were assumptions that may not be realistic?

Indeed, the literature review should culminate with a conclusion of what the gaps were in the existing body of knowledge. This will then form a lead-in to the 'Conceptual Framework of Research' or 'Theoretical Framework of Research' or 'Conceptual Framework of Inquiry'. These will be discussed in further detail in the next section on methodology.

But, what to read?

For research-centric projects, a natural source of information will be the academic journals. The academic supervisors should be able to provide some guide into identifying the journals or even specific papers for the students to get started in this endeavor.

The literature review should also be relevant to practice-based projects. However, instead of relying on academic journals as the primary source of information, the reference sources for practice-based projects can be more encompassing to include periodicals published by professional bodies, reports in various media channels, reports and proprietary papers pertaining to the hosting industry clients, etc.

For related topic, please refer to Chapter 3.

2.9 What is a Conceptual Framework of Inquiry?

We often discuss and debate with friends about policies, preference for certain things or any matter under the sun. For example, we may see a group of friends debating vigorously about which country will win the next FIFA World Cup, or if Singapore should bid to host the Olympics Games. Very often, we call these informal discussions or colloquially coffee shop talks.

But, we can also discuss the same topics in the context of academia, i.e., in classrooms, lecture halls, journal articles, PW reports, etc.

What are the differences between the two?

For a start, it does not mean that the topics discussed in the informal discussions are not serious matters. However, the setting is casual and they are generally not bounded by specific objectives. It also does not really matter whether the discussions lead to any conclusions, consensus or recommendations.

However, PW is a form of academic inquiry. Therefore, the inquiry should be set within a certain framework towards a certain objective. This is called the conceptual framework of inquiry or the theoretical framework of enquiry.

But where does the conceptual framework of inquiry come about? As discussed earlier, this should come from the literature review. In other words, the literature review should conclude with a conceptual framework of inquiry which, depending on whether the PW is research or practice centric, will entail either of the following (Table 2.4):

Table 2.4 Conceptual framework of inquiry.

Type of projects	What the conceptual framework of inquiry will entail
Researchcentric projects	Research questions Hypothesis
Practicecentric projects	Statement of the 'problem' in practice to be solved

2.10 What is the Methodology Chapter for?

While it is true to say every chapter of the report should be equally important, many assessors will agree with us that 'methodology' is the dimension that would and should attract the most scrutiny when appraising a PW report. This is consistent with the earlier discussion about curricular objectives of the PW, in that it is directed at not just testing the substantive knowledge of a specific subject matter, but also the processing skills, i.e., the methodology of inquiry. Unfortunately, it is observed that in a lot of PW reports, this chapter is usually not adequately dealt with to reflect the critical thinking required in this regard.

We cannot over-emphasize the point that the distinguishing factor between an outstanding dissertation and an ordinary one often shows itself from the way the methodology chapter is discussed. Indeed, a good discussion on methodology should demonstrate a rational approach to problem formulation, data collection and data analysis, as shown in Figure 2.3.

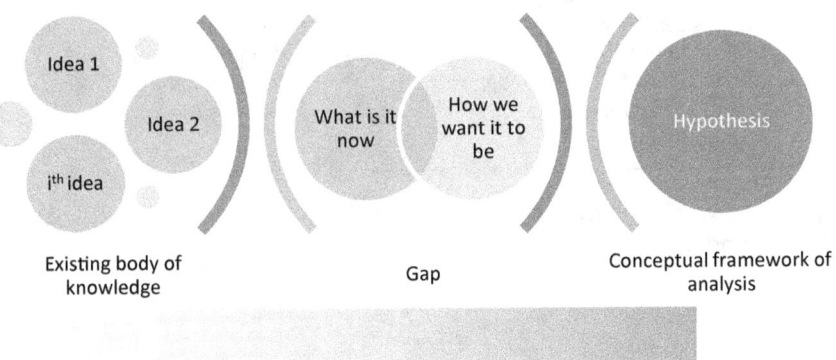

Figure 2.3 The flow of the literature review.

```
┌─────────────────────────────────────────────────────────────┐
│           Introduction Chapter (Problem definition)         │
│  - Choose a title of the project that reflects the essence  │
│    of what it is.                                           │
│  - Explain the key motivation giving rise to the project.   │
└─────────────────────────────────────────────────────────────┘
                              │
                              ▼
┌─────────────────────────────────────────────────────────────┐
│                  Literature review Chapter                  │
│  - Explore what is the existing body of knowledge on the    │
│    subject matter and discuss the potential gaps still      │
│    existing.                                                │
│  - Conclude the literature review with a conceptual         │
│    framework of inquiry. Crystallize from the 'big-picture' │
│    project objective with specific research questions or    │
│    hypothesis.                                              │
└─────────────────────────────────────────────────────────────┘
                              │
                              ▼
┌─────────────────────────────────────────────────────────────┐
│                    Methodology Chapter                      │
│                                                             │
│  A. Discuss the data collection                             │
│     method                              C. Determine the    │
│  - Identify what kind of data and          data analysis    │
│    information is required.                method           │
│  - Explore the few alternative          - This should be    │
│    approaches to gather the data          considered        │
│    and their feasibility with             together with the │
│    reference to the potential             consideration of  │
│    constraints and challenges.            data collection   │
│  - Select a method, which is likely       and the           │
│    to be either quantitative,             development of    │
│    qualitative, or mixed method.          the survey        │
│                                           instrument.       │
│                                         - The methods may   │
│  B. Discuss how the survey                include:          │
│     instrument was developed              - Descriptive     │
│     where applicable                        statistics,     │
│  - Draft the questionnaire.               - Inferential     │
│  - Conduct pilot test and validation.       statistics,     │
│  - Refine and finalize the                - The use of      │
│    questionnaire.                           managerial      │
│                                             analytical     │
│                                             frameworks, or  │
│                                           - A combination   │
│                                             of various      │
│                                             methods.        │
└─────────────────────────────────────────────────────────────┘
```

Figure 2.4 The flow from Introduction to Literature Review to Methodology.

2.11 What are some specific topics that should be included in the Methodology Chapter?

The flow of the methodology chapter may be as follows:

a. State the primary methodology chosen, i.e., whether it is a qualitative, quantitative or mixed method. Explain the rationale for choosing the particular methodology. Elaborate on the key steps you will take to perform the analysis. Please see Chapter 4 for discussions on the techniques for qualitative and quantitative analyses.

b. If the methodology chosen involves the collection of primary quantitative data through a survey, a comprehensive discussion on the matter should include the following:

   i. Sampling. This is almost a necessity in all instances as it is generally impractical to survey the entire population. So, sampling will be necessary. But, this should be methodically done, such as whether it is random, stratified random or other approaches such as purposive.

   ii. Sampling size and its implications on margin of error with respect to an acceptable confidence level. You may use the following or similar sampling tool available in the internet to calculate the sample size required (systems, 2016).

c. If a survey was conducted and a survey instrument (i.e., a questionnaire) was developed for this purpose, discuss how this instrument was developed. There are basically two approaches to do this.

   i. Leveraging on an instrument that was used before, such as the one previously published in a journal. This is a preferred approach unless one is doing doctoral research where originality is very much emphasized. Having said that, one should not just copy. The relevance and choice of the survey instrument thus to be adopted should be critically discussed in the literature review.

ii. Develop a new survey instrument entirely. But, depending on the level of sophistication required, this may entail a lot more effort in validating the instrument, such as the following:

— Checking internal consistency between the main questions and sub-questions. The statistic of Cronbach's alpha may be used for this purpose.

— Checking for questions that have high correlations with other questions, and therefore possibly redundant.

— Using exploratory factor analysis to inspect a preliminary factor structure. Thereafter, using confirmatory factor analysis with a new set of test samples for confirmation of the validity of the survey instrument.

As can be seen, a comprehensive work in this area may entail competency in some specific statistics topics which students may not be trained in. The supervisors may provide guidance on the level of sophistication required which in turn will depend on the level of accuracy required in the surveys. Please refer to textbooks of research methods for in-depth discussions on the design of questionnaires. An example of this is given below:

Burges, T. F. (2001). A general introduction to the design of questionnaires for survey research. University of Leeds. Retrieved from http://iss.leeds.ac.uk/downloads/top2.pdf

2.12 What are the theoretical underpinnings of the methodology applied?

There is a lively debate about the nature of research. The fundamental concepts of ontology and epistemology are introduced and discussed briefly here.

Ontology is concerned with our assumptions about how the world is perceived and how it is researched. There are two very different approaches to this:

a. A realist ontology states that natural laws are ready to be found and researched existing independently of the researcher. Therefore, facts do not depend on social actors to give them meaning. This view is held by positivists (also referred to as objectivists) and is most common in the study of natural sciences.

b. A relativist ontology states that knowledge and therefore research is value-laden, subject to interpretation and social interaction. The world, and particularly the social world, is constantly in flux because its meanings are co-constructed and constantly changing. This view is held by interpretivists (also referred to as constructionists) and is most common in social sciences.

Epistemology is about the relationship between the knower and the known (researcher and researched). In other words, it is concerned with our beliefs about how we might discover knowledge about the world. A main distinction is whether we acquire knowledge through:

a. Rationalism and deductive reasoning

This method works from the more general to the more specific. This is also informally known as the "top-down" approach. We might begin with thinking up a *theory* about our topic. We then narrow that down into more specific *hypotheses* that we can test. We narrow down even further when we collect *observations* to address the hypotheses. This ultimately leads us to be able to test the hypotheses with specific data — a *confirmation* (or not) of our original theories. The process of inquiry is summarised as follows:

Theory → Hypothesis → Observation → Confirmation.

b. Interpretivism and inductive reasoning

Inductive reasoning works the other way, moving from specific observations to broader generalizations and theories. Informally, this is also known as the "bottom-up" approach. In inductive reasoning, we begin with specific observations and measures, begin to detect patterns and regularities, formulate some tentative hypotheses that we can explore, and finally end up developing some general conclusions or theories. The process of inquiry is summarized as follows:

Observation → Pattern → Hypothesis → Theory.

So, how do we make use of the above information?

The above concepts are useful for researchers to explain their selection of the methodology. As an introductory discussion on this rather involved philosophical topic, the summary in Figure 2.5 may help to demystify the concepts:

2.13 What is mixed methods and triangulation?

Triangulation refers to the use of more than one approach to solve a problem or verify the data in the course of doing the PW. There are generally the following four methods of triangulation:

a. Data triangulation — Use different sampling strategies to collect the data.

b. Investigator triangulation — Use another researcher to gather the data. This can be a useful approach to reduce bias. In fact, a good example of the use of this method can be seen in the assessment of PWs whereby the assessment is often done by more than one assessor in order to moderate the effect of bias if any.

c. Theoretical triangulation — More than one theoretical basis may be applied to gather and/or interpret the data. For example, in the evaluation of the financial feasibility of

Structure of The Report/Dissertation/Thesis

		Ontology	
		Realist	Relativist
Epistemology	Rationalism	People who hold a Realist Ontology are known as Positivists or Objectivists. They engage in hypothesis testing guided by rationalism and deductive reasoning. This approach relies on a great number of observations that are repeated to reduce potential effects of variables in order to allow for generalizations. This methodology is generally employed in the study of natural sciences.	
	Interpretivism/constructivism		People who hold a Relativist Ontology are known as Interpretivists or Constructionists. They focus more on how people construct and perpetuate structures of reality through interaction guided by inductive reasoning. This approach relies on observing first and then deriving general conclusions from these observations. This methodology is generally employed in the study of social sciences.

Figure 2.5 Theoretical underpinning of the methodology applied.

a development project, the indicators that can be used for evaluation include Net Present Value, Internal Rate of Return, or the Payback Period. Each of these indicators reflects the financial feasibility of a development project from a different perspective. When used together, they would provide a more comprehensive picture of the whole which would allow better decision making.

d. Methodological triangulation — This may be employed to support multi-dimensional analysis of a problem. Some examples of these are:

— Review and develop a strategic plan or a business plan for an organization: This may include the use of various methods like the surveys, interviews, focus group discussions, SWOT analysis, BCG matrix, financial modeling, etc.

— Conduct a feasibility study for a project:

This may include the examination of the technical, financial, and operational matters associated with the project.

— Review or formulation of a specific public policy:

This may include the use of surveys and focus group discussions for data gathering, the use of scenario planning the identification of the risks and the discussions on the risk management strategies, financial modeling to determine the implications to budgets, etc.

2.14 What should be included in the chapter on data collation and analysis?

This will entail the following three aspects:

a. Presentation of the processed data in an organized manner so that they will become coherent information. It is a good idea to consider using graphs and tables generously to communicate the information.

In addition to the processed information, you may also have a lot of primary data in the form of coding of computer programs, photos, tables of raw data and/or graphs. Some of these need not be included in the report proper. Nonetheless, it may still be good to include them for completeness and for record keeping. In order not to distract the readers from the more critical parts of the PW report, these materials may be included in the appendices of the PW report.

b. Explanation of the theory of the analytical method which you are going to use.

c. Analysis and presentation of the outcome of the analysis, and discussion of the implications of the new findings as either an addition to the existing body of knowledge and/or a solution to issues in practice.

Depending on the flow of the dissertation, it is also possible to discuss the theory of the analytical method which you are going to use as part of the chapter on Methodology.

2.15 What should be included in the Conclusion Chapter?

As the name suggests, the Conclusion chapter should draw the report to a conclusive close. What does this mean? Perhaps, some checkpoints as follows may help:

a. Has the objective as set out in the Introduction chapter been met? Are there any recommendations?

It is very important for the conclusion to address if the objectives of the project have been met.

Furthermore, it is also expected that there should be some recommendations, either for improvements if similar research is attempted in the future, or for potential applications in practice. This is very important as ultimately research should inform potential for further research and/or improve actual practice in the industry.

b. Are there limitations? Have these been discussed?

As discussed earlier, problem solving in research or through models often incorporate assumptions which may not hold in the real world. These are not necessarily defects in the research. Rather, researchers should be cognizant of the impact of these limitations, and interpret the findings with care. Limitations are therefore a very important part of the dissertation which should be discussed. Some limitations commonly cited in PW reports include:

— Larger sample size to be used in surveys.

— Putting together a sample whose composition is more representative of the population.

— Better time management, so that the stages of the project can be completed within the planned schedules.

— Better planning so that the pertinent literatures can be consulted and taken into account in the project.

CHAPTER 3

TECHNIQUES IN REFERENCE SOURCING AND STYLES OF ACADEMIC WRITING

After reading this chapter, you will be able to:

— *Explore and prioritize the sources of information.*

— *Apply strategies for recording information effectively.*

— *Use appropriate linguistic resources for writing academic English.*

3.1 Why must PW involve sourcing for data and information?

Some students may find sourcing for data and information from various sources rather tedious. They may ask if it is necessary to do this at all and whether they can just write a Project work (PW) report based on their own thoughts and opinions. A quick answer to this question is that this is not enough.

Students will need to source for data and information for a combination of reasons, such as the following:

a. Literature review

   This is to find out what is already known about the topic or what related research has already been done previously, i.e. before we embark on the project. This is to ensure we are building upon what has been done previously rather than repeating what is already known. Please read this in conjunction with Section 2.8 on Literature review.

b. Secondary data

   Some times, instead of conducting surveys or experiments to generate primary data for analysis, secondary data can also be a source for research.

   For example, the Singapore Sports Council may conduct annual national surveys on what sports people engage in for exercise. The results and discussions for such annual surveys from a number of years can be collated for longitudinal analysis (i.e., over a period of time). Such collated results can be used for the analysis of whether the popularity of the different sports changes over time (i.e., trend analysis). They can also be used for the analysis of whether there is a relationship between the popularity of a particular sport with changes in income overtime (i.e. correlation analysis).

When such data generated from previous research are used for further analysis as in the examples mentioned above, they are known as secondary data.

Conversely, primary sources are direct or first-hand account about an event, object or a person. They may include historical and legal documents, eyewitness accounts, results of experiments, statistical data, pieces of creative writing, audio and video recordings, speeches, etc. (Ithaca, 2016). Accordingly, primary sources are written by those who

— experienced the event first-hand,
— conducted the experiments and recorded the raw data, or
— conducted the surveys or interviews and recorded the raw data.

In order to determine if the source is primary or secondary, one can ask two questions:

— Has the author constructed the information described from personal experience e.g., as part of an eyewitness account of an experiment?

If the answer to the above is yes, this will likely be a primary source.

— What kind of documentation does the author refer to e.g., Are any other researchers' work referred to?

If the answer to the above is that the data is primarily based on the published work of other researchers, this will likely be a secondary source.

The common sources of information for the various parts of the PW report are shown in Table 3.2.

Table 3.1 Primary and secondary sources.

Primary sources: accounts of contemporary events or original documents	Secondary sources: interpretations of primary sources
— Data and original research; — Diaries and reflective journals; — Letters; — Live speeches and interviews; — Autobiographies; — Government documentation; — Photographs; — Videos of events.	— Biographies; — Chronologies; — Encyclopaedias; — Most journal articles (some data published is primary); published books unless written at the time of depiction.

Table 3.2 Sources of information.

Content	Source
Literate review. Secondary data. Discussion of the results.	From references, such as journal articles, magazines, websites, statistical reports, published by the government, internal management reports of the organizations involved in the inquiry, etc.
Discussions and critique of all the above.	Original writings from the author(s) of the PW report.

3.2 What are useful strategies for finding sources?

Part of the learning objectives of PW is to train tertiary students to learn independently. This is also known as self-directed learning. For this, students will have to learn to look for information and to discern priorities for the selection and inclusion of the more relevant and pertinent sources. Students will have to develop skills in identifying these sources, selecting and organizing them (Figure 3.1).

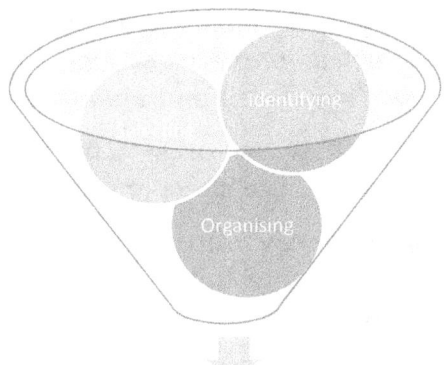

Sources to be included for citation
and/or analysis

Figure 3.1 Funneling process for identifying, selecting and organizing sources to be included for citation and/or analysis.

Important reminder: Students may come across materials which they may find rather sophisticated or impressive. They may want to include them in the literature review or somewhere in the discussions. However, these materials may have nothing to do with the PW report at all. Sometimes, they may just include some diagrams which are not referred to at all in the analysis and discussions. Students are advised not to do this. This will only show their lack of understanding and they may even be penalized.

Two approaches for sourcing the relevant information are discussed below.

a. Using a library website

Conducting a search on a new topic can be daunting. A good start is using a library website. The following are some steps to be followed:

— First, identify keywords for the topic e.g., *socialization*.

— Then, conduct a general search in a subject encyclopaedia to uncover further key terms; in this case, *socialization* in a sociology encyclopaedia leads the researcher to other terms such as *primary* or *secondary socialization* as well as *socializing agents* and *agencies*.

— Students can then use this richer repertoire of key terms to search for the specific references list.

— Examine the title, key words, abstract and the authors' details. Based on this shortlist, proceed to obtain the specific articles or books.

Evaluate all of this information as suggested above before acquiring and reading the whole article. This will help to save a lot of time and effort.

b. Using an internet search engine

Internet search engines are excellent platforms for locating journal papers, newspaper or magazine articles. Some of these platforms are discussed below.

Google Scholar is useful for performing a search. When using this resource, type in at least three keywords. The search should reveal several examples of the source looked for; each comprising the beginning of the abstract and several hyperlinks below indicating other related relevant articles. It is also possible to click on the hyperlink *cited* and choose the APA or MLA (or another if required) to copy and paste into a reference section.[2]

In addition, there are also other online databases that provide collections of subjects, such as EBSCOhost, Gale Power Search, and ProQuest. These online databases comprise some 10,000 periodicals. So, they will be sufficiently comprehensive for researching into various topics.

---

[2] It is advisable to check such auto-generated citations. Occasionally, they may not be complete in which case, it will be necessary to edit them according to the format as suggested in Section 2.4.

Access to such online databases usually entails paid subscription or the payment of a fee on per use basis. However, the libraries for most tertiary institutions should have subscriptions for them in which case, students and staff should be able to access them under the terms as arranged by these institutions.

Authenticating sources:

Evaluating sources also means being able to decide what is appropriate for use in a project.

While online resources from the internet provide a convenient way to source for almost any information needed quickly, easy access to information may dull students' sense of curiosity, blunt critical thinking, and stifle debate. In fact, the over-reliance on internet sources like the Wikipedia may have the opposite effect of promoting shallow rather than deep learning.

Students should strive to heighten their critical-thinking skills. They should avoid just taking in information from the first site returned from an internet search. In fact, with technologies for 'search engine optimization', information that is ranked highly from a search need not necessarily be the most pertinent one. The algorithm for their rankings may have been effected through commercially motivated considerations.

Furthermore, while Wikipedia and similar internet-based resource websites have been found useful by many, they have been criticized for having inaccuracies.

Students therefore need to develop the ability to sift through information gleaned from the internet and discern if they come from serious, refereed work or they are merely anecdotes, shallow ideas or unsubstantiated personal opinions of some individuals.

Thus, as a general rule of thumb, it should be in a university library collection. It should also be dated and the author's name and details should be provided. If not, it might not be adequate for academic research. In addition, sources that are clearly unbalanced with only anecdotal evidence provided are probably unsuitable.

Wikipedia may be used for initial searches. But information gleaned from there should be verified and triangulated against the original sources. Citations should be taken from the original sources wherever possible.

3.3 How can information about a topic be collated and annotated systematically?

One effective method for organizing the vast array of sources is by using a synthesis grid or a synthesis matrix as shown in Table 3.3.

The identification of the sources are listed in the Y-axis. On the X-axis, the dimensions on which the sources are to be analyzed can be used to form the heading (Please refer to Section 3.4 also). Once this grid or matrix structure is set out, notes can be annotated on the squares. The example in Table 3.3 shows the organizing of the various sources for a subject on how athletes tend to morally justify certain behaviors in sports e.g., taking drugs to boost performance or diving in football.

The example of the grid system shown above is just a very simple illustration. The vertical axis can be expanded to include more information so as to suss out useful and relevant information for the literature reviews or discussions of the results. Such further details may include:

a. Summary of the source in:

— What is the purpose in framing the investigation? This refers to the broad area of the research.

Table 3.3 Synthesis grid.

Source.	Boardley, I. J. & Grix, J. (2014). Doping in bodybuilders. *Qualitative Research in Sport, Exercise and Health*, 6:3, 422–439.	Corrion, K., Long T., Smith, A. L., Arripe-Longueville, F. (2009). Athlete Accounts of Moral Disengagement in Competitive Sport. *The Sport Psychologist*, 23, 388–404.
Moral disengagement techniques.	Bandura: social cognitive theory.	Bandura: social cognitive theory.
Competitive or non-competitive sports environment.	Non-competitive.	Competitive.
Presence of technique.	All 8 mechanisms present in bodybuilders.	All 8 mechanisms present in Taekwondo and basketball.
Results of technique as related by psychologists.	Very effective. However, existing research suggests the timing of doping interventions may be a critical consideration; periods of career instability appear to be a point at which athletes may be particularly vulnerable to doping practices (Mazanov et al., 2011).	Very effective but distinction between moral disengagement in competitive and non-competitive sports found.

- What is the primary objective of the research? How does this research add to the research?
- What are the theoretical framework and the methodology used?
- What are the results?

b. Assessment of the source:

- Why is it a good bibliographic source? How does it relate to other sources in the bibliography?

c. Reflection on the source's limitations (if any):

- What is its limitation?
- How is that problem being dealt with?

3.4 What are useful strategies for mapping out the big picture?

There are several academic strategies for developing and recording knowledge about a topic. The concepts of mind-mapping and concept mapping are discussed in this section.

a. Mind-mapping

A mind map is a diagram used to visually display how the mind may receive and organize information. It can be used to generate, visualize, structure, and classify ideas, and as an aid to studying and organizing information, solving problems, making decisions, and writing.

A mind map is often created around a single concept, drawn as a word or an image in the centre of a blank piece of paper. Thereafter, associated ideas such as images, words and parts of words are added and extended from it.

Major ideas are connected directly to the central concept, and other ideas branch out from them.

Mind maps can be drawn by hand. It is a useful tool to help the formulation of the initial ideas and connect them to the bigger picture. Whil some may choose to refine the mind map until it reaches the final one, it is not always necessary. As mentioned earlier, mind maps may be used as an intermediate output or as a means to an end.

Tony Buzan is credited as the originator of mind maps. He proposes the following guidelines for constructing a mind map (Buzan, 2013):

— Begin in the middle of the page with a word or image.
— Short, concise key words or phrases should be used, not too many wordy sentences.
— Each part of the map should be connected to the centre and the lines should become thinner as they move away from it.
— Different colors can be used to code or group ideas to aid memory.

Mind-mapping software can be used to structure information and to organize it hierarchically. Software packages can also be exploited to construct links between documents such as spreadsheets or even internet sites.

b. Concept mapping

Concept maps have their origin in the learning movement called constructivism. In particular, constructivists hold that learners actively construct knowledge by building on and linking information as they are exposed to it.

A concept map is a diagram that shows relationships between concepts. It helps students to develop logical

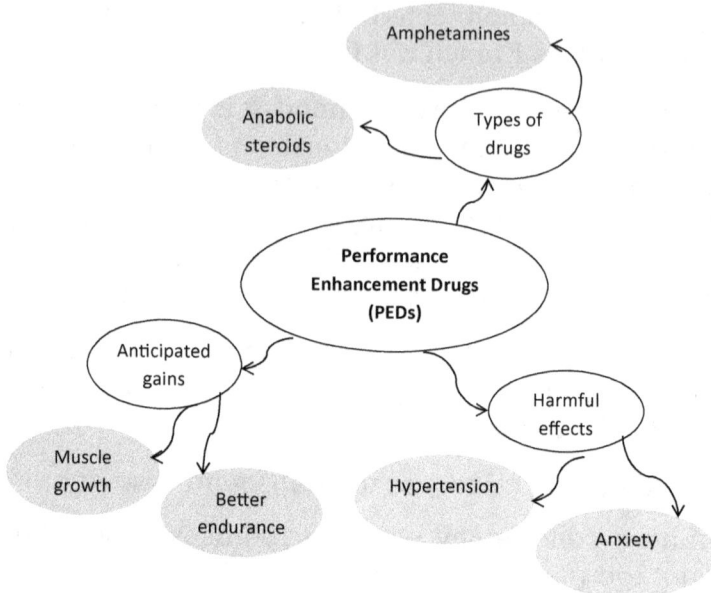

Figure 3.2 Example of a simple mind map.

thinking by making connections amongst concepts explicit. In doing so, students appreciate the individual ideas that form a larger whole.

A concept map is often defined by an explicit focus as is the mind map. Ideas and information are provided and are connected with labeled arrows producing a hierarchical structure. The relationship between concepts can be articulated in linking phrases such as *causes, requires,* or *contributes to*.

Figure 3.3 shows a concept map representing relations between concepts with regard to Performance Enhancing Drugs (PEDs) in sports.

c. Comparison lists

Comparison lists allow the student to compare related topics. Here is a simple overview of the nature/nurture debate and its relation to socialization in sports studies (see Figure 3.4).

Techniques in Reference Sourcing and Styles of Academic Writing **75**

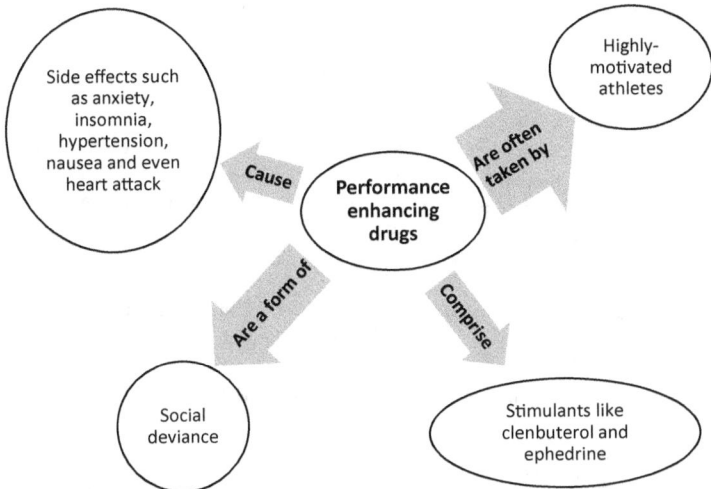

Figure 3.3 Example of a simple concept map.

3.5 How should sources be used in academic writing?

You may read this in conjunction with Section 2.7 regarding Literature Review.

Good academic writing depends on the use and evaluation of multiple information sources. Using other sources gives academic writing an authoritative voice and a high level of persuasion. The terms used to cite and assess other authors are *attribution* and *authorial endorsement or dis-endorsement*. These strategies are most commonly carried out using reporting verbs such as *state, argues, posits* shown as in the example which provides neutrality:

> 'Giulianotti *states* that social theories help us to understand sport today.'

A writer can also evaluate and demonstrate agreement or disagreement with an author using reporting strategies. This is

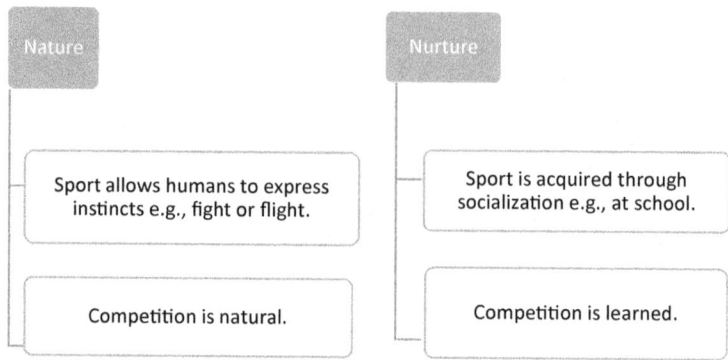

Figure 3.4 A comparison list.

known as authorial endorsement and authorial disendorsement; examples:

— Endorsed: X demonstrates...

— Strongly endorsed (SE): X convincingly demonstrates ...

— Disendorsed: X claims...

— Strongly disendorsed: X wrongly claims...

Apart from using adverb + verb structures, adjective + nouns may also be used. An example sentence applying this structure is:

> Savulescu (2004) has provided highly cogent arguments as to why doping is in fact not against the spirit of sport.

The grammar of reporting verbs falls into two basic patterns:

— The first is reporting verb + noun; example:

  'Coakley (2009) *confirms* Gramsci's theory......'

— The second is reporting verb + that + clause; example:

'Coakley (2009) *demonstrates that hegemony theory* can be applied to the emergence of sport cultures such as skateboarding.'

Attribution and endorsement are normally carried out using the present simple tense as in the examples above. However, it is common to use the past tense when discussing the methodology and results of prior research; example:

'The interventions *carried* out during the research ....'

3.6 What are some guiding principles for effective academic writing?

It is difficult to provide an all-encompassing answer to this question but generally, a good writer should do the following:

— Present the research purpose precisely and completely;

— Build relevant, logical, and fair arguments;

— Express ideas clearly;

— Cite relevant evidence to support a position;

— Accurately grasp the point of view of another author or speaker;

— Identify, understand, and evaluate the assumptions underlying someone's position;

— Reasonably assess the credibility of an author;

— Recognize and evaluate evidence and key assumptions on both sides of an argument;

— Use appropriate field-specific language;

— Use general academic language appropriately;

— Order the different parts of a text and build logical relationships between these parts effectively;

— Use grammatically accurate language throughout.

3.7 What is grammar and how is it important in academic writing?

Grammar is a set of conventions for organizing language so that they are used consistently and convey consistent meaning.

In recent time, a lot of people are used to writing emails, texting or instant messaging. Most of the time, these are written in informal language, where errors in grammar are often overlooked.

In academic writing, it is absolutely essential to write in a grammatically correct manner. This is especially important when students are expected to convey understanding of complex matters.

The ensuing sections in the remaining part of this chapter will focus on styles in academic writing as well as some of grammar which have been observed to be particularly challenging for students who are more accustomed to speaking or writing in an informal style.

3.8 What is cohesion in academic writing?

One of the commonly encountered problems with PW reports is that the ideas of the sentences or paragraphs do not flow. As a result, they appear rather disjointed or incoherent to the readers. This can be a major defect as it may indicate weakness of the thought process and/or inadequacies in written communications.

In linguistics terms, this is an issue of 'cohesion', which refers to the way in which a text 'hangs together' linguistically so that all the parts link up and make sense. Indeed, writing cohesively is a crucial aspect of academic writing.

While the techniques highlighted here may be subtle, they can go a long way to enhance the quality of writing, and hence communicate the ideas more effectively. Supervisors can also refer to the examples provided here to trigger the students to consider how they can apply the techniques in their own writings.

In a nutshell, the cohesion of the PW reports can be enhanced with 'devices' to thread a text together. This method was originally outlined by two linguists, Halliday and Hasan, in their classic work on cohesion in 1976 entitled "Cohesion in English". In this introductory discussion on cohesion, we would like to highlight five key cohesive devices commonly implemented in written academic texts.

a. Reference

This looks at the way in which words refer directly to other words in the text. There are three types of references, i.e., anaphoric, cataphoric and exophoric references as elaborated below.

i. Anaphoric

This is to refer backwards to an item that has been mentioned earlier.

Example:
'*Sport* allows humans to express instincts. *It* is in part related to spontaneous actions of fight or flight.'

The pronoun '*It*' is an anaphor; it points to the left toward its antecedent '*Sport*'.

Example:
'The football match stopped, and *that* upset everyone.'

The demonstrative pronoun *'that'* is an anaphor; it points to the left toward its antecedent *'The football match stopped'*.

ii. Cataphoric

This is to look forward to an idea that the writer will elaborate in the later part of the sentence or the next few sentences.

Example:
Using *their* knowledge of cohesive devices, *effective readers* can quickly construct meaning from text.

The possessive adjective *'their'* is a cataphor; it points to the right toward its postcedent *'effective readers'*.

Example:
In *their* free time, *the school boys* play video games.

The possessive adjective *'their'* is a cataphor; it points to the right toward its postcedent *'the school boys'*.

iii. Exophoric

An exophoric reference or an exophor refers to something that is not directly present in the text, but is rather present (like alluded to) in the situational context. An exophoric reference therefore directs us to a context that we are familiar with. It is assumed by the writer to be shared knowledge.

Example:
The business world was shocked by the recent investigations.

The demonstrative adjective '*The*' is an exophorS; it is taken for granted that the reader knows what the business world refers to in this sentence.

Example:
This car is better than *that* one.

The demonstrative adjectives '*This*' and '*that*' are exophors; they point to entities in the situational context.

b. Substitution

Here, a word is used as a substitute for a word, phrase or clause.

Example:
It is a useful tool to help the formulation of *the initial ideas* and connect *them* to the bigger picture.

The noun '*the initial ideas*' is substituted by '*them*' instead of repeating it.

Example:
'Which design would you like? I would like the *one* with the yellow trim'.

The word '*one* is used instead of repeating '*design*'.

c. Ellipsis

Here, instead of words being replaced by another word, the words are missed out completely. The omitted words are 'taken as read'. It would, in fact, be possible to insert them into the text. Ellipsis is sometimes called 'zero substitution'.

Example:
One *strategy* to help students to develop logical thinking is concept mapping, another ( ) is a comparison list.

The word '*strategy*' is missing in the second part of the sentence. But the sentence is also complete without this word. It is taken as understood.

d. Conjunction

A conjunction is used to relate two clauses. They are extremely useful in critical thinking and writing. Students will likely find these notions very helpful in putting forward their arguments, especially in Literature review and in discussing the findings.

They are generally used in five ways as shown in Table 3.4.

Table 3.4 Conjunctions and their usage.

Usage of conjunction	Examples
Additive–to reinforce an argument.	Furthermore; In addition
Adversative–to counter an argument.	However; In contrast
Concession–to express that something is unexpected or surprising.	Despite; In spite of
Causal–to indicate the cause and effect.	Consequently; As a result
Temporal–to indicate some sort of sequence.	After that; Finally

e. Lexical Cohesion

In lexical cohesion, words that are related to each other semantically are used in conjunction with one another. There are several forms of lexical cohesion. Please see discussions below.

i. Word repetition
This is generally used for reiteration. At times, repeated words are used instead of using pronouns 'it' or 'that' in order to minimize confusion.

Example:
The student is working on a <u>research</u>. This <u>research</u> is very innovative.

ii. Synonym

A synonym is a word or phrase that means exactly or nearly the same as another word or phrase. They may be used to elaborate or reinforce the meaning of the conjure.

Example:
This invention is very *innovative*. It is *ground-breaking*.

iii. Antonym

Antonyms are generally regarded as word pairs whose meanings are opposite to another.

Example:
Instead of *fearing stress*, he *embraces* it during a match.

iv. Hypernym and hyponym

Hypernyms and hyponyms are related words where the hypernym is superordinate (i.e., above, encompassing), while the hyponym is subordinate (i.e., below).

Hyper–means above; therefore hypernym is a generic word that can apply to the original word and others (similar to a category).

Hypo–means below; therefore hyponym is more 'drilled down' or more specific from the original word.

Example:
Football, golf, tennis are kinds of *sport.*

Sport is the hypernym, while '*Football, golf, tennis*' are the hyponyms.

Example:
To *research* the topic, you may '*read, interview, observe,*' etc.

In the above, '*research*' is hypernym, while read, interview observe are the hyponyms.

A word may be a hyponym in one context, but a hypernym in another.

Example:
Living things comprises *birds*, insects, fish and mammals. '*Birds*' is a hyponym here.

Example:
Birds comprise different spices like sparrow, hawk, crow, fowl, etc.

Bird is a hypernym here.

3.9 How do I construct a noun group and what is nominalization?

First of all, let us clarify what a noun is. A *noun* is a word that functions as a name for groups or categories of things, such as persons, animals, places, things, etc. Please see examples below.

Person:

> She is the *person* you should consult.
> Michael Jordan is a famous *basketball player*.
> Her *brother Karl* was a very gentle soul.

Animal:

> A *dog* can have fleas but a flea can't have dogs!
> *Elephants* have effective long-term memories.
> Young *horse*s will learn nothing if they are subjected to a bumping match every time they run.

Place:

> The site of the oblong piazza is Domitian's ancient *stadium*.
> The Gunners play *there*.
> Paris and London are two beautiful *cities*.

Things:

> He showed excellent awareness of the *ball*.
> I select this *sentence* as its pertinent summation.
> The *association* arranges mixed tournaments in *tennis* and *golf*.

Idea:

> Follow the *rules*.
> Newton's laws of motion were major scientific discoveries.
> *Love* is a wonderful emotion.

Nouns are also organized into different groups in accordance to their form, function, and meaning. Knowing these will provide us with the confidence to leverage on the different usage of nouns to communicate our thoughts more clearly.

Abstract noun:

> This is a noun that names a concept; example: evidence, information, knowledge. It is also known as a non-count or mass noun and is used in singular form. These nouns almost never occur with an 's'; example: anger, love, integrity, faith, hope, joy, calm, reality, etc.

Concrete noun:

> It depicts a material object that the senses can experience. It is also known as a count noun and is used in singular and plural forms; example: experiment(s), division(s), activit(ies).

Attributive noun:

> It functions as an adjective and co-occurs with other nouns; example: university degree, research project.

Collective noun:

> It depicts a group of individuals; example: committee, government. These can co-occur with singular or plural pronouns depending on whether the group is viewed as a single unit or not.

Denominal noun:

> This is formed with a suffix; example: experimentalist, computerization.

Deverbal noun:

> This is constructed by adding -er/-or to a verb; example: researcher, translator.

Verbal noun

> This is also known as gerund. It is derived from a verb using the suffix –ing; example: eliciting, exploring.

However, sometimes we may need to describe certain things more clearly with the use of more words. In such instances, we may form a noun group. Hence, a noun group is a group of words depicting an entity; for example:

> '*The nice old English police inspector who was sitting at the table* is Mr. Morse'.

The portion in italic in the sentence above is the noun group. This noun group becomes the subject of the sentence. It can be seen from this example that the structure of a noun group can comprise determiners or modifiers which modify the description of the head noun, which is the inspector in this case. The modifiers can be in the form of numerals, adverbs, adjectives as well as nouns. They can be placed before the head noun (pre-modifiers) or after the head noun (post-modifiers).

The flexibility for noun groups to be formed allows a great deal of meaning to be condensed into the subject or the theme of a clause. This helps to make English versatile, and easy to use for science and technology.

Please see further examples below.

Examples of head nouns with pre-modifiers:

An   *increasingly*   *expanding*   *market.*
(Determiner)   (Adverb)   (Adjectival clause)   (headnoun)

The headnoun '*market*' has been modified with modifiers '*An increasingly expanding*'.

The   *second*   *best*   *Sprint*   *Time.*
(Determiner)   (Numeral; ordi-   (Adjective)   (Noun)   (Head-
              nal or cardinal)   noun)

'*Sprint*' and '*Time*' are the noun and headnoun respectively. Their meaning has been modified with modifiers '*The second best.*'

Examples of head nouns with post-modifiers:

A   *major*   embarrassment   to the school
(Determiner)   (Pre-modifier)   (Head word)   (Post-modifiers)

The headword '*embarrassment*' has been modified with modifiers '*major*' and '*to the school*'.

New   conceptual analysis   based on contemporary research.
(Pre-modifier)   (Head word)   (Post-modifiers)

The headword conceptual analysis has been modified with modifiers 'New' and 'based on contemporary research'.

The   results   providing the absolute proof.
(Determiner)   (Head word)   (Post-modifiers)

Techniques in Reference Sourcing and Styles of Academic Writing   89

The headword 'results' has been modified with modifiers 'providing the absolute proof.'

Noun groups are also used in-lieu of verb phrases. Specifically, the grammatical process of changing a verb (or an adjective) into a noun is nominalization. Please see example below.

> Original sentence: "Many more people *are playing in* mixed gender sports these days."
>
> Verb phrase "*are playing in*" is expressed as noun phrase "*an increase in participation in*".
>
> After the change: "There has been *an recent increase in participation in* mixed gender sports."

3.10 Should I use active or passive voice in academic writing?

The active voice is direct (subject–verb–receiver), vigorous, clear, and concise. The active voice emphasizes the 'doer' (i.e., the subject) of the action. The reader knows who carried out the action.

On the other hand, the passive voice is indirect (receiver–verb–subject). The passive voice emphasizes the receiver (or product) of the action. Very often, the subject may not even be mentioned at all. They can be perceived as weak, awkward, and wordy.

Examples:

Active voice:

> I think there is a significant difference between Group A and Group B.

Smith *et al.* investigated the relationship.
We have analyzed the results.
The organizer concluded that the event is a success.

Passive voice:

It is observed that there is a significant difference between Group A and Group B. Plant seeds are dispersed.
The relationship was investigated.
The results have been analyzed.
It is concluded that the event is a success.

While active voice has been recommended in general writing for the merits it possesses, in academic writing, passive voice is more commonly adopted. The reasons include the following:

a. We want to focus on the objective outcome rather than the one doing the action. Passive voice allows writers to highlight the most important participants or events within sentences by placing them at the beginning of the sentence.

   Example:
   'The *data* suggests that the mutation causes cancer.'; instead of saying:
   We believe the mutation causes cancer.

   The focus is on the subjective matter of the *data* rather than the authors themselves.

b. In order to avoid irrelevant or repetitively stating who the 'doer' is.

   Example:
   'With the data collected, the regression analysis will be performed.'; instead of saying,

Techniques in Reference Sourcing and Styles of Academic Writing

"I will perform the regression analysis with the data collected."

It is obvious that the author will be the one doing the analysis.

Example:
'The samples were selected via stratified random sampling based on the height ranges of the athletes. Invitations to attend the interviews were sent to the athletes via emails. Briefing was conducted before the start of the interviews.'; instead of saying:

'I have selected the samples via stratified random sampling from the athletes of different height ranges. After that, I have also sent invitations to attend the interviews via emails. Before the start of the interviews, I have also conducted briefings."

There were unnecessary focus and repetitions on the doer'. Writing in passive voice can make the sentence more elegant.

c. As passive voice does not name the 'doer', the meaning or tone of the passive sentences will sound more diplomatic and less aggressive.

Example:
'It is unclear how the earlier researchers have carried out the sampling of the athletes in different height ranges. Hence, the issue of integrity of the samples have remained unaddressed.'; instead of saying:

'I disagree with the earlier researchers with the way they carried out the sampling. Specifically, they have also not explained how the samples from the athletes in different height ranges have been selected.'

By using the passive voice, the focus is on the objective matters rather than the individuals. This should be the spirit in the writing of an intellectual discourse.

A final word of advice on this matter is that debate between active and passive voice is not a matter of right or wrong. It is more a matter of choice. For academic writing, the reasons for the preference for passive voice is as discussed. Notwithstanding that, there are some academic publications which encourage the use of active voice. Thus, for those who are seeking to write for publication, it is necessary to follow the guidelines of the publishers concerned.

3.11 What is Subject-verb agreement?

A verb is a word used to describe the following:

— A physical action. Example: He <u>conducted</u> the experiment.

— A mental action. Example: She <u>formed</u> the conclusion.

— A state of being. Example: She <u>possesses</u> the knowledge and skill to design a car.

A subject is part of a sentence. It is the word that refers to a person or thing that is being discussed, described, or dealt with. As discussed earlier, this kind of words are nouns rather than verbs.

A common problem observed in students' writings is that the subject and the verb in a sentence do not correlate. Students need to be sensitized to this and rectify this problem.

Verbs must correlate with their subjects. Singular and plural verbs should have singular and plural subjects.

Subjects can be in any of the following forms:

— Simple nouns. Example: The <u>research</u> concluded that ...

— Pronouns. These are words like <u>he, she, they, their</u> and a few others that replace nouns so that one do not need to keep repeating the nouns. Example: The players have completed the training programme. <u>They</u> have done well.

— Noun groups. This is a cluster of words around a noun used to indicate a person or a thing. Example: The sports industry, the university lecturers, the under-15 team, etc.

— Complex noun groups with a head noun. Example: The ground-breaking *research techniques* (compound noun as head) developed; or

— Complex pronoun groups. Example: *All of the experiments conducted* have provided the same results.

Sometimes it can be difficult to identify the head noun or pronoun of the subject. Here are some examples:

The <u>application</u> of mixed methods research in corporate organizational structures has led to a much better understanding of the effectiveness of teambuilding activities such as corporate retreats.

From the above example, it is evident that the head noun does not need to be the closest to the verb. To work out which noun is the head, it is important to ask who or what the verb refers to; in this case, what has led to a better understanding?

Each of the strategies developed has provided a boost to the economic development policies of local government.

From the above example, it is evident that the head pronoun refers to each <u>one</u> of the strategies. Therefore it correlates with a singular verb. Pronouns that act in the same way are *either, every, neither* and *none*.

A plural verb is used if two or more singular head nouns are joined with *and*.

> Example:
> Both Germany and Brazil have won the FIFA world cup more than three times.

However, a singular verb is used if two singular head nouns are joined with *or* or *nor*.

> Example:
> Either Germany or Spain will win the FIFA World Cup in 2018 in Russia.
> Neither Greece nor the Ukraine has held the FIFA World Cup.

Some can correlate with both a singular or plural verb depending on whether the noun is count or noncount.

> Example:
> Some drinking water was found to be polluted at the stadium.
> Some players have complained about their working conditions.

A plural verb is used with few and a singular with little.

> Example:
> Few scientists have yet to condone germ line therapy for the future of sporting super athletes.

Pronouns that act in the same way are *both, many, some* and *several.*

> Example:
> Little research has explored whether germ line therapy is safe beyond the first generation.

Pronouns that act in the same way are *much, some, no.*

> As noted above, there are many collective nouns including *committee*; government; team; community; population; majority; minority. These co-occur with singular or plural pronouns depending on whether they are viewed as a single or plural unit.

> Example:
> The team has been playing relatively badly recently.
> The majority of South Africans have embraced each other's differences.

Many nouns that end in *'s'* correlate with a singular verb:

> Example:
> Athletics; biomechanics; economics; politics; robotics

As noted above, many nouns are noncount (*evidence, information, knowledge, research*). These never occur with an *'s'* and are always singular.

3.12 What is hedging?

When discussing results from research, we may want to suggest a possible explanation to a phenomenon or a potential solution to a problem. These are mere suggestions rather than conclusive certainties.

How do we do that? The technique to do this is called hedging in linguistics. It refers to the use of modality in academic

Table 3.5 Examples of hedging.

Types of hedging	Examples
Lexical verbs	The results *suggest* that … The research *indicates* that …
There or it + lexical verb	There *seems to be* evidence that … It *appears* that …
Usuality adverbs	Often, frequently, usually, occasionally
Probability adverbs	Clearly, evidently, probably, possibly, incontrovertibly
Modal auxiliary verbs:	*May* suggest, *might* show, *could* develop, *would* demonstrate
Modal adjectives	Certain, doubtful; evident, clear, probable, possible
Modal nouns	Assumption, probability, possibility, doubt, indication
Modal verb + that clause	It might be the case that … It could be suggested that …
It + (modal verb) + be + adjective + infinitive with to	It may be necessary to research … It is important to study …

writing. Modality is the meaning space between 'yes' (positive polarity) and 'no' (negative polarity). It removes certainty from propositions. It is commonly construed using a variety of linguistic resources. Please see Table 3.5 for some examples.

3.13 What is affixation?

A morpheme is the smallest meaningful unit in a language (Katamba, 2005, p. 29). Some morphemes carry meaning on their own and cannot be broken down into smaller units, e.g., child; pay; happy. These are referred to as free morphemes. Others do not carry meaning on their own. These are bound morphemes. They perform a lexical or grammatical function either by making new words (lexical) or changing a word from

Techniques in Reference Sourcing and Styles of Academic Writing 97

one part of speech (grammatical) to another. Suffixes and prefixes are bound morphemes. That means, similar to the grammatical suffix *-s* to make nouns plural or the *-ing* to change a verb's meaning, they can only occur with another morpheme, specifically, a free morpheme. The prefixes and suffixes presented in this section carry lexical meaning.

a. Suffixes in English change parts of speech; example:

— adding *less* to *hope*; it changes the noun to an adjective *hopeless*;

— adding *ly*, which changes an adjective to an adverb (*mistakenly*);

— adding *ment*, which changes the verb *pay* to a noun *payment*.

It is very useful to know some of these suffixes. The following is a useful list of suffixes for use in academic English:

Noun-forming suffixes: er; ment; ness; ion

Changing verbs to nouns; example:

box-er; train-er; agree-ment; govern-ment

Changing adjectives to nouns; example:

effective-ness; spontaneous-ness

Changing adjectives to nouns; example:

educate-ion; act-ion

Verb-forming suffixes: -en; -ify; -ize/ise

Changing adjective to verb; example:

wide-en; short-en

clear+ify — clarify; specific+ify — specify

Adjective — Forming Suffixes: able; full; less

Changing verbs to adjectives; example:

predict-able; understand-able

Changing nouns to adjectives; example:

market-able; profit-able

use-ful, bounty-ful

use-less; meaningless

Changing nouns to verbs; example:

Memory+ize — memorize; valor+ize — valorize

Changing adjectives to verbs; example:

local-ize; modern-ize

Adverb-forming suffixes: ly

Changing adjectives to adverbs:

clear-ly; demonstrative-ly

b. Prefixes in English except en- (en- changes the adjective live to enliven) do not change parts of speech. They create new meaning or new words.

un- (not) + adjectives forms new adjectives or + verbs to form new verbs; example:

un-able; un-aware; un-over; un-tie

in- (not) + adjectives forming new adjectives; example:

in-accurate; in-efficient

dis- (not) + adjectives forming new adjectives; example:

dis-similar; dis-advantageous

a- (not) + adjectives forming new adjectives; example: *a*-moral; a-typical

re- (again) + verbs forming new verbs; example: re-construct; re-arrange

dis- (not) + verbs forming new verbs; example: dis-allow; dis-continue

mis- (wrong) + verbs forming new verbs; example: mis-direct; mis-understand

pre- (before) + verbs forming new verbs; example: pre-arrange; pre-select

in- (not) can in some cases occur with nouns; example: in-balance; in-decision

dis- (not) + nouns forming new nouns; example: dis-advantage; dis-harmony

Table 3.7 presents the other most common prefixes in academic English to form new verbs:

Table 3.8 presents some of the other most common prefixes in academic English to form new nouns:

For an extensive presentation of the affixes found in English, please refer to English language Roots (2016) and Root worked lesson (2016).

Table 3.6 Examples on the use of adverb forming suffixes to form new verbs.

Suffix	Meaning	Example
al	action/result	Survival
-able	can	Presentable
-ship	state of being	Fellowship
-age	collection of	Collage
-ity	state	Velocity
-cy	state	Efficiency
-age	result	Coverage

Table 3.7 Examples on the use of prefixes to form new verbs.

Prefix	Meaning	Example
bio-	life	biography
chron-	time	Chronology
co-	together	Co-locate
doc-	teach	Doctrinally
equi-	equal	Equi-distance
fore-	before	Foreword, foreground
grav-	heavy	Gravitate,
hyper-	over	Hypertension, hyperactive
inter-	between	Inter-school, inter-disciplinary
out-	better than others	Outstanding, outlasting, outperform,
over-	too much	Overarching,
sub-	below	Subsurface,
trans-	across	Transpacific, Transcontinental
un-	opposite	Unable, unknowingly
under-	not enough	Underperform,

Table 3.8 Examples on the use of prefixes to form new nouns.

Prefix	Meaning	Example
min-	small	Miniature
mono-	one	Monolingual, monorail
neo-	new	Neoclassical
over-	excessive	Overburden
pop-	people	Population
post-	after	Post-war, post-modernism
pseudo-	false	Pseudonym, pseudolatry
semi-	half	Semi-final, semi-detach
simil-	like	Similitude
sub-	below	Substructure,
super-	above	Superstructure,
sur-	above	surcharge
tele	distant	Telephone
tri-	three	Trimaran, triangle
ultra-	beyond	Ultra conservative
under-	below	Underestimate
vice-	deputy	Vice-President, Vice-Chairman

3.14 How do I punctuate academic English correctly?

The most common devices used to punctuate academic English are commas, semi-colons, colons and apostrophes.

a. Using commas (,)

   i. To list

   Example:
   A shop selling apparels wants to decide how it should prioritize amongst formal business suits, informal business wear, casual or sports apparels.

ii. To sequence a sentence (*first* and *first of all* can also be used in this way)

Example:
There are two main reasons for not legalizing performance enhancers. First, they are dangerous. Second, athletes who do not use them, might feel coerced into doing so.

iii. To join a dependent and an independent clause

Example:
Once Bannister had breached the 4-minute mile boundary in 1954, it was broken again two months later by him and Landy.

b. Using semi-colons (;). These function half-way between a comma and a full stop

i. To link two independent clauses that are closely related

Example:
Track and field competitions in the 19th century were typically contests between rivals at educational institutions; these meets were first regularly held at Exeter College, Oxford.

ii. To link opposing independent clauses together

Example:
The NFL is a sport known for its concussions and other serious injuries; nonetheless, it is still one of the most popular sports in America.

iii. To list

Example:
The following authors wrote on the American Civil War: Woodworth, Steven. E; Eicher, David J; and Murdock, Eugene C.

c. Using colons (:)

   i. To introduce a list

   Example:
   The following authors wrote on the American Civil War: Woodworth, Steven. E; Eicher, David J; and Murdock, Eugene C.

   ii. To create a thematic flow in a text

   Example:
   Some argue that the sport society we have today has shifted from: it's not about winning but how you play to whatever it takes to win.

d. Using apostrophes (')

   Contractions (e.g., don't, haven't) are not appropriate in formal writing. Hence, apostrophes (') can only be use for indicating possession.

   i. Regular singular noun

   Example:
   The footballer's boots

   ii. Regular singular noun that ends in the letter s (e.g., *cactus; lens),* grammar advocates the use of another s.

   Example:
   The bus's occupants were delayed;
   Jones's house ...

   iii. Singular compound noun.

   Example:
   Participant-researcher's view

iv. Regular plural noun, add an apostrophe after the s.

   Example:
   The teachers' meeting room ...
   The actresses' scene ...

v. Irregular plural nouns (e.g., nucleus, tooth) that change their form when pluralized the *s* follows the noun similarly to regular singular nouns.

   Example:
   The teeth's formation ...
   The nuclei's center ...

vi. Plural compound noun.

   Example:
   Participant-researchers' views ...

vii. Compound nouns with prepositions (e.g., in; of; with):

   Example:
   Sisters-in-law's speeches ...
   Mothers-with-child's waiting room ...

viii. Two or more subjects own the same object.

   Example:
   Halliday and Hasan's book on linguistics ...

ix. The possessions are separate.

   Example:
   Halliday's and Hasan's books have had a great impact on research in linguistics.

3.15 Where can useful sources to develop academic writing be found?

There are a lot of online sites that can be used for independent study and as reference sites for input on effective academic writing. Some of these as listed below:

— University of Harvard: http://writingprogram.fas.harvard.edu/

— University of Sydney: http://writesite.elearn.usyd.edu.au/

— University of North Carolina: http://writingcenter.unc.edu/handouts/evaluating-print-sources/

— University of Victoria: http://web.uvic.ca/wguide/Pages/StartHere.html

— Purdue University: https://owl.english.purdue.edu/

CHAPTER 4
SELECTION OF METHODOLOGY

After reading this chapter, you will be able to:

— *Determine which method you will employ for your Project Work (PW).*

— *Perform some basic qualitative and quantitative analysis.*

4.1 How to consider the choice of methodology of a project?

The choice of the methodology is central to the overall design of a project. This has to be considered upfront during the design phase of the project. A frequently observed situation is that students only start to think about the methodology in depth a lot later after the project has started. At that time, if the originally intended methodology is found not feasible and it is too late to change, the project may be badly affected.

The starting point to consider the methodology of a project is the objective. This in turn has to be considered in conjunction with the issue of whether the project is research centric or practice centric. Flowing from that, the specific types of investigation and the corresponding analytical techniques will have to be considered. Please see Figure 4.1.

The common types of investigations are elaborated below:

a. Observation-based projects

   In observation-based projects, the researchers will try to observe a phenomenon without interfering in it. These are normally used in social sciences, such as in action research or the study of organization behavior.

   In such projects, the definition of the research problem may be more broadly stated. They may also be exploratory in nature. For example, a project to 'analyze decision making processes in the planning and organization of the Olympic Games'. The project will likely entail the investigator reviewing internal correspondences, minutes of meetings, and observing proceedings of meetings. Additional queries may also arise during the course of the study. He or she may notice unusual happenings and decide to probe 'What is happening?' or 'Why?'.

Selection of Methodology

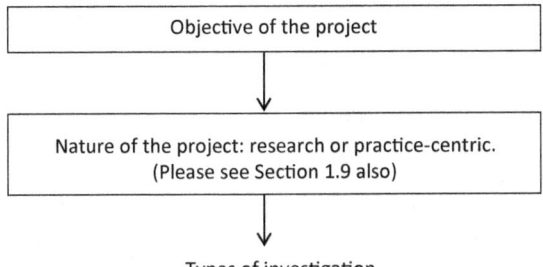

Type	Remarks	Primary analytical techniques
Observation-based.	Usually used in social sciences, such as in action research or the study of organisation behavior.	Descriptive and qualitative.
Opinion-based.	These will involve the collection of data through surveys, interviews, Focus Group Discussions or a combination of these.	Qualitative and/or quantitative.
Experiment-based.	Experiments are set up within laboratory or at the field for the collection of primary data for analysis.	Generally quantitative.
Review of previous works.	Such studies are aimed at reviewing and critiquing earlier studies with the hope of synthesizing new insights. The data will be based on pre-existing secondary sources.	Qualitative and/or quantitative.
Proof of Concept.	For demonstrating the feasibility of a concept, which can be a physical product, policy, organizing an event or a business model. This is frequently used in conjunction with design thinking.	Qualitative and/or quantitative.

Figure 4.1 Systematic process of consideration in the selection of the methodology of a project.

Observation-based projects may also be used as a precursor to further in-depth studies involving more specific research questions and/or quantitative methods. This kind of project design may also be useful for studies where the interventionistic approaches are not desirable due to ethics considerations.

b. Opinion-based projects

Opinion-based projects will involve the collection of data through surveys, interviews, focus group discussions or a combination of these. The common types of projects that adopt this approach may be market research, satisfaction surveys, opinion surveys, etc.

While data collected from interviews and focus group discussions will likely to be qualitative in nature, results from surveys may be subject to quantitative analysis. For a start, such results may be analyzed and discussed with their descriptive statistics like mean, standard deviation, or presented via graphs.

c. Experiment-based projects

In experiment-based projects, experiments are designed and set up to collect data and subject these to quantitative analysis of the variables. Relative to the observation-based projects, the research questions will likely to be more specifically stated, such as in hypothesis testing.

A very important aspect of experiment-based projects is the issue of repeatability. In other words, if the experiment thus designed is repeated in the future, they should yield similar conclusions.

Set-ups for experiments are by definition artificial. These are designed to simulate or represent aspects of the phenomenon in the real world. As such, some approximations or assumptions may have been included as part of the experiment design. It is important for the investigator to take these into considerations when discussing the results.

d. Review of previous works

By definition, meta-analysis is a kind of studies aimed at reviewing and critiquing critical points of earlier studies with the hope of synthesizing new insights. Naturally, the data will be based on pre-existing sources, which can be from published works or internal documents of the subject organization involved in the study. Besides scrutinizing such data, further analysis may also be performed on them.

Example: A series of sports event satisfaction surveys may have been conducted for a number of sports events over a period of time. Meta-analysis may be performed by aggregating such data from such previous studies on individual events to analyze if there are difference amongst indoor or outdoor events, or individual or team sports, or if there are changes in trend over time.

As meta-analysis does not involve the collection of primary data from surveys or experiments, it is often done as a desktop study.

e. Proof of Concept

Proof of concept projects are usually practice-centric. They may also be known as prototyping.

Proof of concept can be used for demonstrating the feasibility of a concept, which can be a physical product, policy, organizing an event or business model. Accordingly, they are usually done with a limited scale. The principles of design thinking will be most relevant here.

Depending on the nature of the subject matter, such projects may be built upon quantitative and qualitative analysis techniques, or the use of engineering or financial management principles.

4.2 What are quantitative and qualitative analysis?

There are two categories of techniques to analyze a problem. These are quantitative and qualitative.

a. Quantitative analysis

As the name suggests, quantitative analysis involves the collection, compilation and analysis of numbers within the subject matter of statistics. The specific techniques range from simple display of descriptive statistics to sophisticated ones like structural equation modeling.

Hence, this is a big subject of study by itself. Depending on nature of the projects, students who would like to sign up for projects involving quantitative analysis should have some prior training in statistics.

b. Qualitative analysis

On the other hand, qualitative analysis relies on the collection and analysis of non-numerical data. Such data are mainly verbal data in text rather than measurements. The information gathered is then analyzed in an interpretative, subjective, impressionistic or even diagnostic manner.

In this chapter, a few commonly used analytical methods in PW are discussed. The introductory discussions here are intended to help students appreciate what these methods are so as to help them decide which technique to use. If students want to study in detail how to use the methods, they are encouraged to consult the statistical books and/or other resources available on the internet, or attend the pre-requisite courses as may be prescribed by the institution.

4.3 What should be presented in an analysis with descriptive statistics?

What is it?

This is the simplest form of quantitative method and is easiest to understand. It involves primarily the compilation of data and presenting them with bar chart, pie chart, etc. You can explore the different attributes of the different chart types so that you can select the ones to best communicate the information. Some examples of the commonly used charts are shown in Figures 4.2A–4.2J.

Figure 4.2J demonstrates the use of the technique of normalization. This is also part of the overarching methodology of ratio analysis routinely used in the finance industry.

In this example, due to a wide variation of the population size of countries involved in the South East Asian Games, it is difficult to make a meaningful assessment of which country has performed better by simply comparing the total number of medals won. This is because countries with larger populations will have a higher chance of winning more medals simply because they have more people to choose from to compete in the games. Hence, normalization allows comparisons to be made on a more equal footing.

What normalization does is that, instead of using the raw data of the total medals won by each country directly, this number is divided (i.e., normalized) by its population to derive the ratio of 'Medal per million population' as shown in the vertical axis.

Likewise in the horizontal axis, the GDP of the country has been normalized by dividing its gross GDP by its population. In this example, although the economy and hence the GDP of larger countries like Malaysia is larger than a small country like

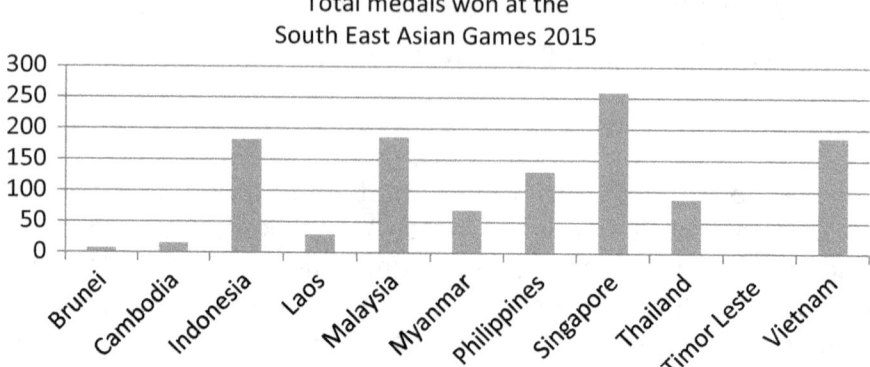

Figure 4.2 (A) A simple bar chart.

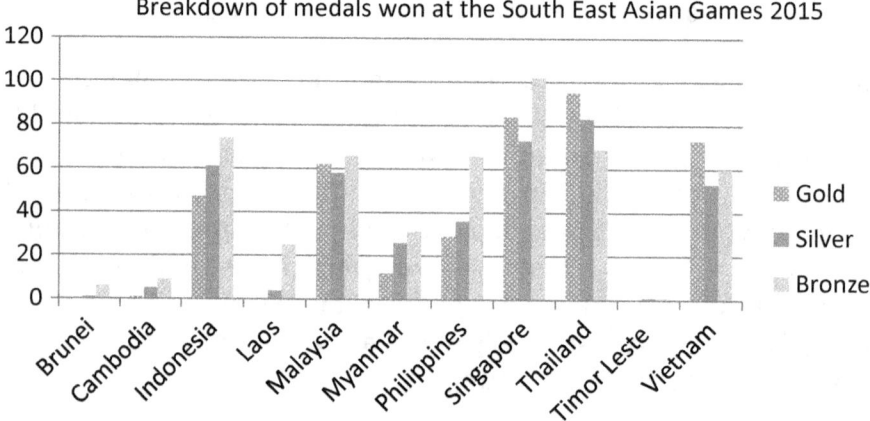

Figure 4.2 (B) A compound bar chart. Relative to the simple bar chart, the compound bar chart can be used to show multiple indicators of each item along the X-axis. In this example, it is able to display the breakdown of medals into Gold, Silver and Bronze.

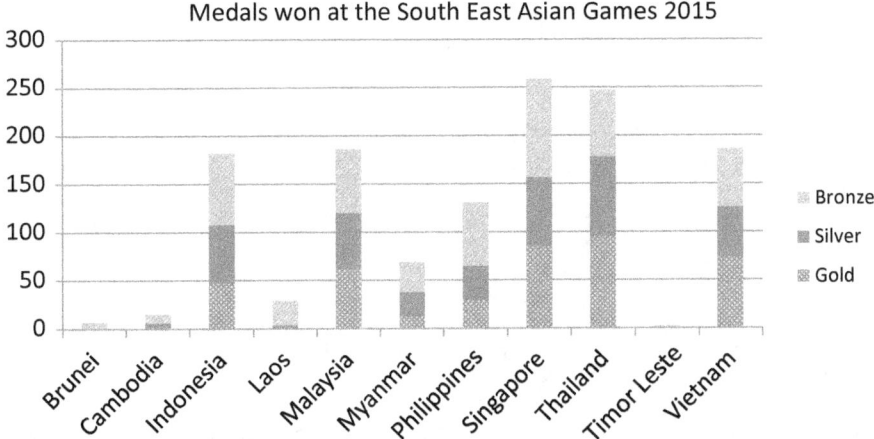

Figure 4.2 (C) Stacked bar chart. This is a variation of the compound bar chart shown in Figure 4.2B. Not only can this chart be used to show the breakdown of the different types of medals, it can also indicate the total number of medals won by each team.

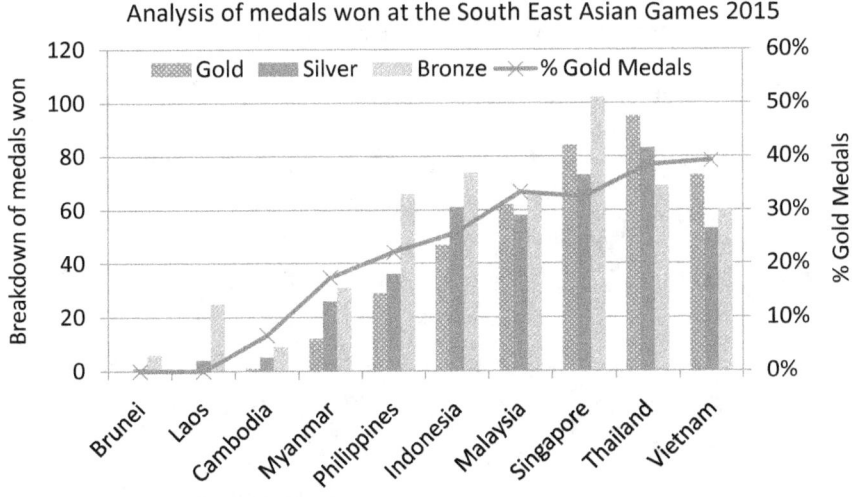

Figure 4.2 (D) Bar chart with two vertical axes. In this example, the number of gold, silver and bronze medals is shown with respect to the vertical axis on the right. Whereas, the vertical axis on the left shows the percentage of the total medals of each team that are gold medals.

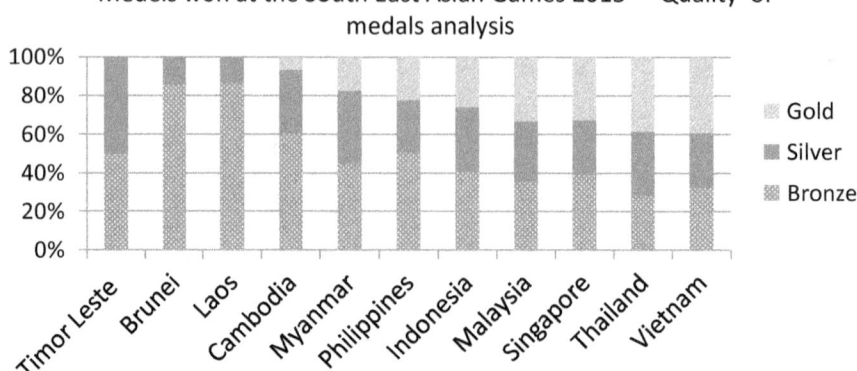

Figure 4.2 (E) This is a 100% stacked bar chart. Pay attention to the difference between this and the normal stacked bar chart shown in Figure 4.2D. The vertical axis of this chart is expressed as a percentage instead of the absolute number, hence it adds up to 100%. In this example, it can be used to discuss the 'quality' of the medals earned in terms of the percentage of medals won that were gold.

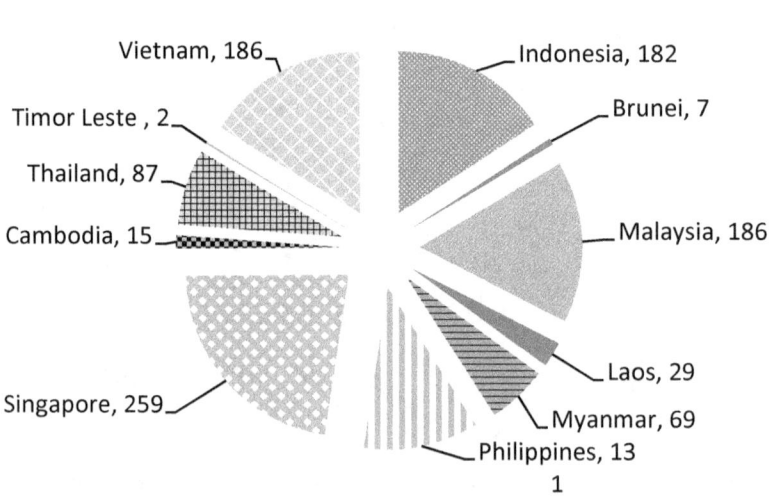

Figure 4.2 (F) A pie chart. This is an alternative to the simple bar chart. Pie charts are useful to present simple information about proportions, but they have limited scope for presenting more complex information.

Selection of Methodology

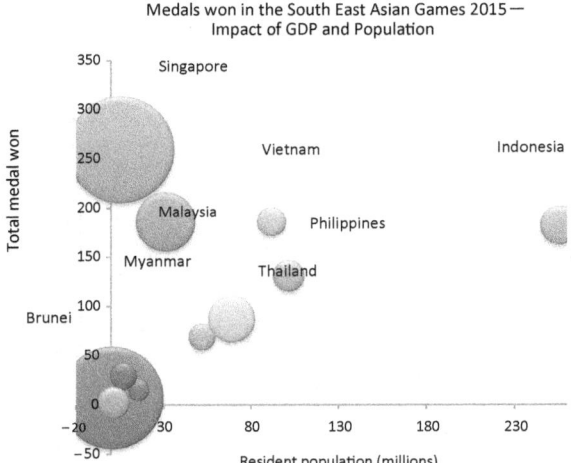

Figure 4.2 (G) This is an example of a bubble chart. The bubble chart is visually impactful for being able to simultaneously display information from three dimensions, i.e., the x-axis, the y-axis, and the diameter of the bubbles. This would support a rich analysis to be discussed. In this example, the size of the bubbles represents the relative size of their Gross Domestic Product (GDP) in Purchasing Power Parity (PPP) in USD.

Figure 4.2 (H) This is a radar chart. The visualization provides different kinds of insights not provided by the other chart types. In this example, it shows the different kinds of sport in which the counties excel in. It also shows that the bulk of the medals are provided in swimming and athletes. Thus, countries that focus on these two sports will tend to achieve similar good performances on an overall basis.

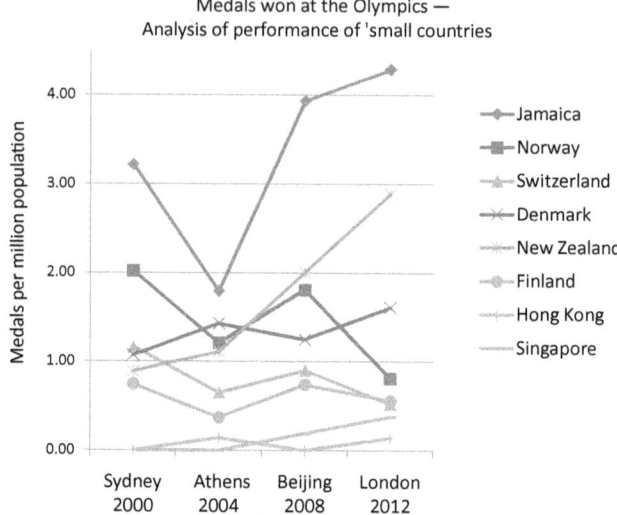

Figure 4.2 (I) This is a line chart. In this example, it shows how the achievements of some selected 'small countries' change over time. The analysis of the change of certain phenomenon over time is frequently used. This is also called trend analysis.

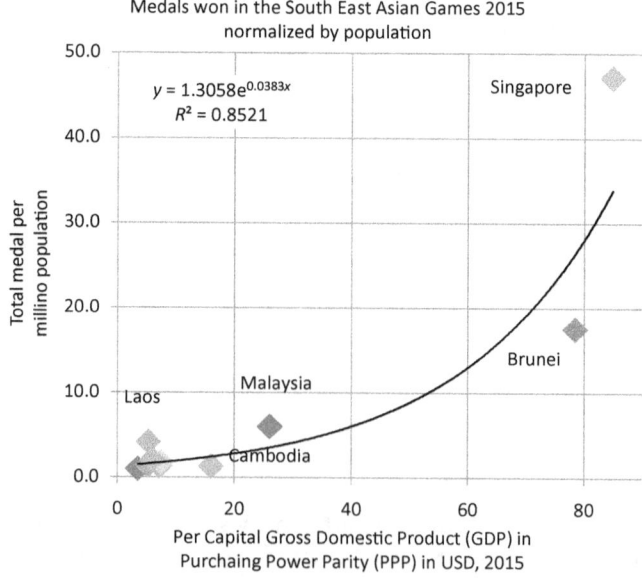

Figure 4.2 (J) A scatter plot with regression and correlation analyses. Please see Table 4.1 for the corresponding tabulated data.

Table 4.1 Analysis of medals won with normalization.

	GDP PPP (USD) 2015	Total Metal	Medal per mil pop	GDP per capita PPP (USD) 2015	Population (mil)
Brunei	31	7	17.5	78.5	0.4
Cambodia	54	15	1.0	3.5	15.5
Laos	37	29	4.1	5.3	7.0
Malaysia	812	186	6.0	26.1	31.1
Myanmar	270	69	1.3	5.2	51.9
Philippines	740	131	1.3	7.3	101.4
Singapore	467	259	47.1	84.9	5.5
Thailand	1108	87	1.3	16.1	68.8
Timor Leste	9	2	1.7	7.5	1.2
Vietnam	550	186	2.0	6	91.6
Indonesia	2836	182	0.7	11.1	255.5

Brunei, on a GDP per capita basis, Brunei will have more resources to cater to its smaller population.

Hence, through the technique of ratio analysis in general and normalization in particular, we are able to derive deeper insights into the phenomenon. In this example, students may conclude that the per capita GDP of a country will have a positive impact on its sporting performance in international competitions. This observation can be reinforced with the regression and correlation analysis as will be explained later. In order to substantiate this quantitative observation, students investigate further by doing more literature review to explore potential explanations of this phenomenon. They may find that a potential explanation is that countries with high per capita GDP may be able to devote more resources to support the training of the athletes over a long period of time. They may be able to afford participations in more overseas training and competitions, or they may have a lower coach to athlete ratio such as each coach can focus on the training of few athletes.

In addition, Figure 4.2J also demonstrates a scatter chart which has been augmented with regression and correlation analysis. While this topic will be discussed in Section 4.5 later, some explanations and observations on the use of these techniques are discussed here to help students appreciate how easily they can be used and the significant insights they can generate:

— A trend line obtained by linear regression has been added to the chart. The equation of the trend line is shown at the top left-hand corner of the chart. The R^2 value which is an indicator that shows the 'goodness of fit' of the regression line to the data points is also shown. In this instance, the R^2 score of 0.85 is relatively close to the perfect fit score of 1. It shows a reasonably high goodness of fit of trend line to the data points.

— Additionally, the coefficient of correlation between the vertical axis (Medals per million population) and the horizontal axis (Per capita GDP) is computed to be 0.89. This is a reasonably high correlation, which is relatively close to the perfect correlation score of 1.

In addition to presenting charts, the following basic descriptive statistics are also useful to be presented and discussed as they communicate a lot about the nature of the data:

a. Mean, μ: This is the simple average of all the data points.
b. Median: This is the point where 50% of the data points will fall under or above it.
c. Standard deviation, σ: This indicator describes how the data points are spread out. The larger the standard deviation, the more spread out will be the data.

For example, the height of a class of students ranges from 155 cm to 181 cm. The mean height is 169 cm. The standard deviation is plus or minus 6 cm.

In cases where the data points are eventually spread out like in the normal or near normal distribution, the mean and median may not differ much (Figure 4.3A). However, where the data points are skewed, it will be useful to examine the median in addition to the mean in order to get a more accurate appreciation of the situation. When the data is positively skewed, the median will tend be larger than the mean (Figure 4.3B). Conversely, if the data is negatively skewed, the median will tend be smaller than the mean (Figure 4.3C). This situation occurs quite frequently in the debate on economic policies. Governments will usually cite the high Mean salary of the workforce to argue that its economic policies are effective. On the other hand, the opposition will counter argue that there are a lot of lower income people that cause the distribution to be negatively skewed. Hence the Median, which is lower than the Mean will be more reflective of the true situation.

When is it used?

This approach is frequently used for presenting survey results in market research or opinion polls. You can frequently see them in newspapers and magazines.

Although simple and seemingly unsophisticated, the value of this method is not diminished. It is perfectly fine for PWs to employ this approach for their quantitative analysis. But, students should not just narrate the obvious. For example, instead of just saying that a certain graph shows the sales of sports merchandise has increased by 50% between 2010 and 2015, students should also make an attempt to offer potential explanations. In this case, the increase in sales could be due to the increased interest in sports as a result of Singapore hosting mega sports events during this period, such as the Youth

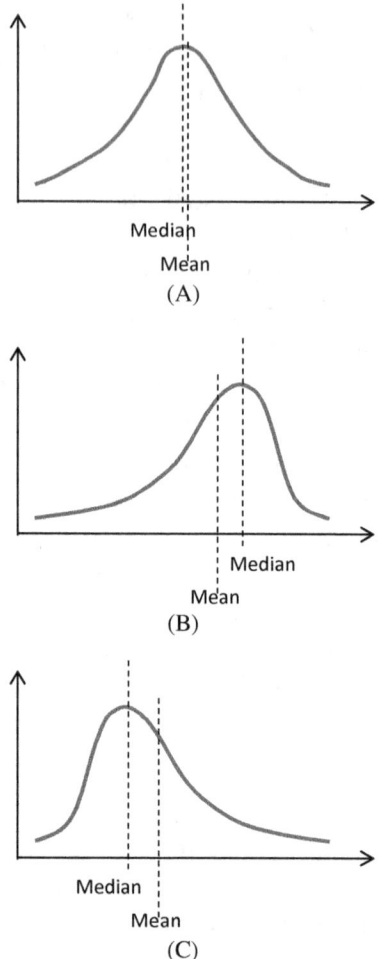

Figure 4.3 (A) Effect of negative skewness on mean and median. (B) Effect of positive skewness on mean and median. (C) Effect of negative skewness on mean and median.

Olympic Games 2010, WTA Women Tennis 2014, SEA Games 2015, etc. This way, the student can demonstrate his or her critical thinking skills as well as ability to apply information from different sources to analyze and explain a phenomenon.

What further analysis can be done?

If similar surveys have been repeated with PWs in different semesters, trend analysis may be performed. The authors can observe and discuss how the descriptive statistics seem to be changing, if the mean is increasing or decreasing over a period of time, which can be monthly or yearly. They can also discuss the potential implication of such trends.

4.4 What is hypothesis testing?

When to use this method?

Hypothesis testing is often used to determine if there is significant difference between two sets of data. For example, a sports apparel company has designed a new swimsuit that will allow people to swim faster. It wants to find out if it is indeed effective. It can conduct an investigation with ten swimmers. In the first instance, the swimmers will be asked to wear the new swimsuit to swim. Their timings will be recorded. Thereafter, the swimmers will be asked to change to their normal swimsuit to swim. Their timings will be taken again. The same procedure can be repeated the next day but with the sequence exchanged, i.e., swimmers will swim with the normal swimsuit first and then the new swimsuit. This is to even out the effect of tiredness, where swimmers may swim slower in the second instance due to tiredness.

The two sets of timings are then compiled. They can then be used for hypothesis testing to determine if there is any significant difference between them. If there is a significant difference, we may conclude that the new swimsuit does have an effect on the ability of the swimmers to swim faster.

What are the steps of doing hypothesis testing?

Step 1: State the hypotheses.

This involves stating the null hypothesis H_0 and alternative hypotheses H_1.

The null hypothesis H_0 is where you commence the hypothesis testing. This is the basic assumption that there is no difference in the averages of the two sets of data being tested, or that the difference between them is not significant. In the example here, the null hypothesis H_0 is that the new swim wear does not make any difference to the swimmers' timing. In other words, the mean of the first set of data should be the same as that of the second set, i.e., $\mu_1 = \mu_2$.

On the other hand, the alternative hypothesis H_1 is the opposite of the null hypothesis H_0. It represents the notion that the two sets of data being tested are different. In other words, the difference of their mean is significant. In the example here, the alternative hypothesis H_1 can be stated as one of the following:

a. μ_1 does not equal μ_2. In other words, μ_1 can be greater (>) or less than (<) μ_2. Since there are two possibilities, the test that will be conducted will be called the two-tailed test.

b. $\mu_1 < \mu_2$. In this case, you will be testing only one scenario, i.e., if μ_1 will be $< \mu_2$. Hence, this will be a one-tail test.

c. $\mu_1 > \mu_2$. Similar to the case above, you will be testing only one scenario, i.e., if μ_1 will be $> \mu_2$. Hence, this will also be a one-tail test.

Please see Figure 4.4.

As can be seen above, hypotheses are stated in such a way that they are mutually exclusive. That is, if one is true, the other must be false.

Step 2: Formulate an analysis plan.

After you have set up the hypothesis, you can then proceed to set the criteria and conduct the testing of the data collected. This will be done by computing and observing the value of the 'test statistic' which is sometimes denoted with the letter 'T'. The attributes of 'T' are summarized as follows:

Selection of Methodology

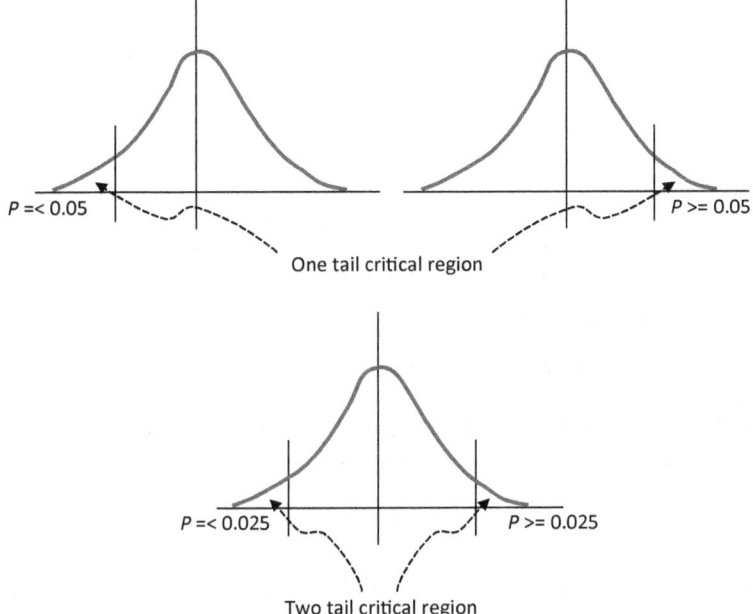

Figure 4.4 One-tail and two-tail tests.

a. '*T*' is a number that describes the attributes of the difference between the two sets of data sample.

b. '*T*' is not a single absolute number. It is a probability distribution function. Please see Figure 4.5.

c. Specifically, '*T*' indicates how many standard deviations an element is from the mean. This can be seen clearly in the definition of one of the 'test statistics', the Z-statistics:

$z = (X - \mu) / \sigma,$

Where:
X = Mean of the sample.
μ = Mean of the population.
σ = Standard deviation of the population.

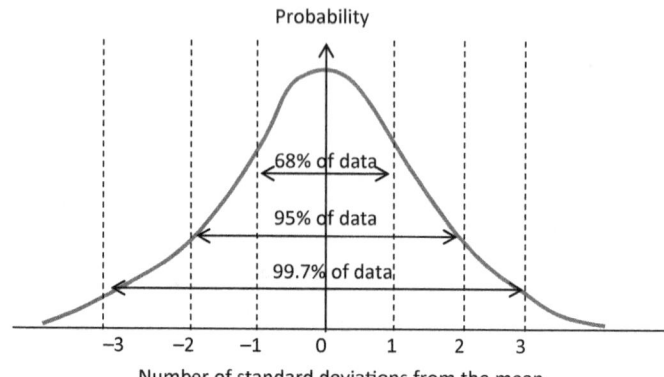

Figure 4.5 Relationship between probability (*P*-value) and the standard deviation in a density function of a normally distributed 'test statistic' '*T*'. *Source*: LTCC (2016).

Bearing in mind how the hypotheses have been set out, the objective of the hypothesis test is therefore to examine if '*T*' is statistically significant or not. In other words, you will want to find out the probability that '*T*' will fall as close as possible to 'zero', in which case, the null hypothesis H_0 can be accepted.

An easy way to express the above notion is in terms of the number of standard deviations from the mean. Please see Figure 4.5 which shows a normal distribution with the *x*-axis representing the number of standard deviations from the mean.

The test criteria that was mentioned earlier is precisely the probabilities mentioned here. The objective of the test is therefore to determine in which zone the 'T' occurs, which in turn will tell us what the standard deviation is.

Basically, depending on the size of the sample and the nature of their distributions, there are several test statistics you may use:

a. Student *t*-test. This is frequently used to compare if there is significant difference between two statistical populations.

b. Z-test. The Z-test is similar to the t-test. Both tests assume the data from the two groups are independent. The differences are in the following:

— The z-test is based on the normal distribution, whereas the t-test is based on Student's t distribution. The t-test is used when the sample standard deviation is not the same as the population standard deviation, when the sample size is small (for example, less than 30), and when the variance of the sample is unknown.

— The t-distribution has somewhat fatter tails.

— The t-distribution varies depending on the number of subjects, but the z-distribution does not.

Step 3: Make conclusions about the hypothesis

After the test statistic has been computed, you will compute the P-value. The P-value indicates that the probability or the extent of the distribution of the two sets of data will overlap.

Figure 4.5 which shows the probabilities of 'T' falling within various standard deviations from the mean under the normal distribution:

a. The probability of 'T' falling within one standard deviation of the mean is 68%.

b. The probability of 'T' falling within two standard deviations of the mean is 95%.

c. The probability of 'T' falling within three standard deviations of the mean is 99.7%.

Thus, if the p-value is large, say 0.95, this means there is 95% chance that the distribution of the two sets of data overlaps. You may conclude that the two sets of results are basically similar. In other words, you accept the null hypothesis H_o.

Table 4.2 Type I and Type II errors.

	H_0 is true	H_1 is true
Accept H_0	Right decision	Wrong decision Type II Error
Reject H_0	Wrong decision Type I Error	Right decision

In hypothesis testing, the objective is to accept or reject a hypothesis based on the pre-determined criteria. However, in so doing, it involves a risk that a wrong decision may be made, not so much due to the computational errors on the part of the students, but more due to the nature of the data available for computation. Such errors are known as Type I and Type II errors and are explained in Table 4.2.

Where either H_0 is accepted or rejected and this decision is correct, it means the decisions taken on the samples are truly applicable to the entire population. Conversely, the cases of errors arise when one decides to retain (or reject) the null hypothesis based on sample calculations, but that decision does not really apply for the entire population. Students who use hypothesis testing should bear this in mind. They may raise this issue in the discussions on interpreting the results or limitations.

Please refer to An Example of a Hypothesis Test (2016) for more details.

4.5 What are correlation and regression analysis?

This is to determine the extent to which two variables (say, X and Y) are correlated with one another. In other words, you want to know when one variable changes, to what extent the other variable will change correspondingly.

Some examples of their applications are given below:

a. In a company, when the salaries of employees (X) are increased over a number of years, whether it can be observed that the profits (Y) of the company show corresponding increase over the same period.

b. In a university, when the funding (X) for research projects are increased over a number of years, whether the number of patents filed (Y) show corresponding increase over the same period.

c. The government would like to find out if decreasing the tax rate (X) will lead to higher economic growth rates (Y).

d. The Minister in charge of sports would like to examine if increasing funding (X) to the National Sports Associations (NSA) to help them conduct better training programmes will have any effect on the number of medals (Y) won in international competitions.

Correlations are indicated by the Coefficient of correlation, typically denoted by the system 'R'.

The R value is computed via a formula involving X and Y which are the two variables being examined. The computation can be done conveniently with statistical software or simply Microsoft Excel.

The following are the interpretations of the value of R:

$R = 0$, X and Y are totally not correlated. This means, when X changes, there is no bearing on any corresponding changes in Y. Please see Figure 4.6A.

$R = 1$, X and Y are perfectly linearly correlated. This means, when X increases for a certain amount, Y also increases by the same amount. Figure 4.6B shows a strong correlation that is close to $R = 1$.

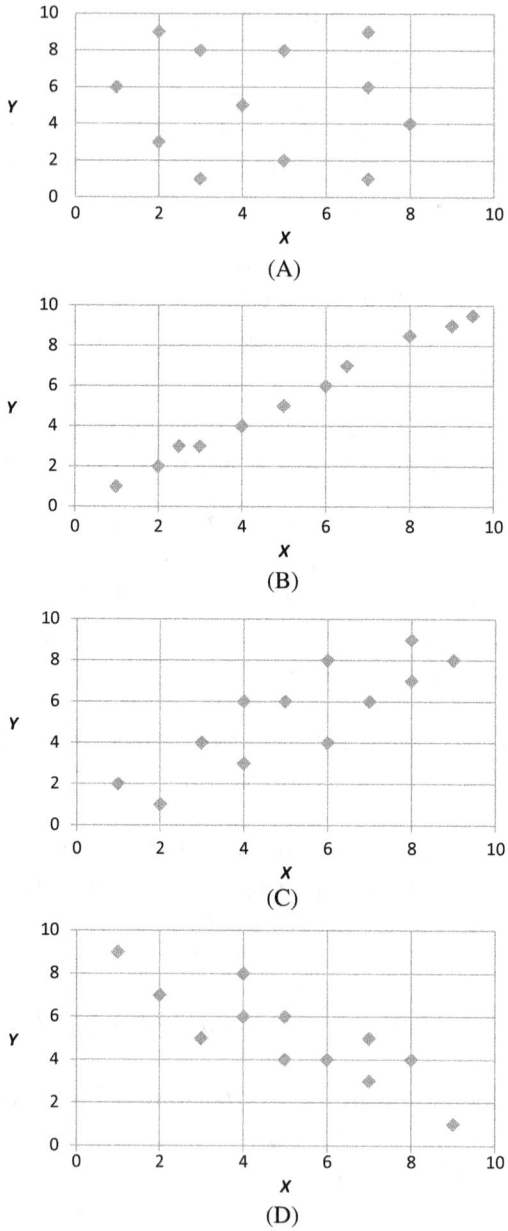

Figure 4.6 Graphical representation of various levels of correlations. (A) No correlation. (B) Strong correlation. (C) Visible positive correlation, but not as strong as Figure 4.6B. (D) Negative correlation.

If $0 < R < 1$, it indicates there is some correlation between X and Y. The closer R is to 1, the stronger is the correlation. Please see Figure 4.6C for a case of visible positive correlation though this is not as strong as Figure 4.6B.

But, R may be a negative value. In which case, the two factors X and Y are negatively correlated. This means, when X increases, Y decreases, or vice-versa. Please see Figure 4.6D.

Correlation analysis is a powerful tool. But, there are some limitations. Some of these are:

a. Correlation does not completely tell us everything about the data. Means and standard deviations continue to be important.

b. The data may be described by a curve more complicated than a straight line, but this will not show up in the calculation of R. Polynomial regression may help to address this to some extent. If you are using Excel to plot the best fit curve, you can specify if you would like to fit a linear or a polynomial graph.

c. Outliers may have a strong influence on the R value. If there are outliers in the data, we must be careful about what conclusions we draw from the R value.

d. Just because two sets of data are correlated, it does not mean that one is the cause of the other. We can only say they are correlated.

If the correlation is found to be significant, then it may be of interest to find out the best possible equation that will describe their relationship. This can be done by using regression analysis.

Regression analysis is to find the best fit curve that describes the relationship between two variables in the form of an equation:

$y = mx + c$, if it is a straight line, or

$y = ax^2 + bx + c$, if it is a polynomial to the power of 2.

However, the usefulness of the coefficient of correlation will depend on how the data points are spread. To express this notion, the statistic Goodness of Fit usually denoted by 'R^2' is used.

Basically, the following observations can be made:

$R^2 = 0$, all the data points are scattered evenly.

$R^2 = 1$, perfect fit. All the data points fall on the regression line.

If $0 < R^2 < 1$, it indicates there is some degree of fit. The closer R^2 is to 1, the closer is the fit to perfection.

How is regression analysis useful? If we know X and we want to predict what Y will be, we can substitute X into the equation to find Y. Thus, regression analysis is very powerful as it provides us with the equation with predictive ability.

But, we must be mindful that even though the equations can be computed mathematically, their validity in practice may be

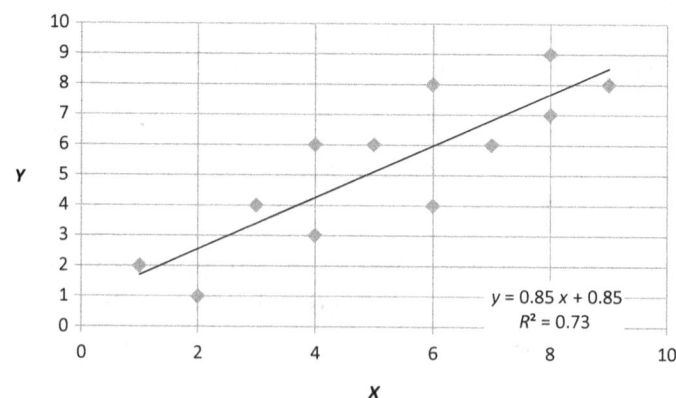

Figure 4.7 A trend line is added to the graph in Figure 2.10C earlier. The equation of the trend line and the R^2 value are also shown. This plot can be generated by the Excel software easily.

subject to various limitations. One of which could be that the equations may only be valid within a certain range of X or other conditions.

Students should therefore develop the appreciation of the meaning of the outcomes of statistical analysis rather than just being able to compute them with the use of computer software.

Correlation and regression analysis can be performed with Microsoft Excel quite easily. More involved analysis may be performed with the IBM SPSS software. Please read more about this predictive analytic software from the website provided below.

Please read discussions on Figure 4.2G earlier and also refer to IBM (2016a) for more information.

4.6 What is Structural Equation Modeling?

The Structural Equation Modeling (SEM) is an advanced statistical technique for solving complex problems. It is more commonly employed in doctoral and post-doctoral level research. In a very simplified manner, the SEM can be considered to be a sophisticated version of regression analysis where many variables can be analyzed together within a network of relationships contained in a mathematical model.

An important first step in performing an SEM analysis is to hypothesize and construct a model using paths or systems diagrams. Thereafter, data is put into the model for the analysis to be performed.

As this involves complex and repeated calculations, computer software will be needed to support this type of analysis. One computer software that supports SEM is IBM SPSS Amos. This software is also owned by the IBM. You can read more about it from the IBM (2016b).

4.7 What are the commonly used qualitative analytical methods?

Qualitative research is commonly used in social science. This type of research focuses on how individuals and groups view and understand the world and construct meaning out of their experiences. It is generally narrative-oriented rather than involving calculations (Office of National Statistics, 2016).

Some of the methods under the umbrella of qualitative research include: ethnography, ethnology, oral life history, case study, focus groups, conversation analysis, and portraiture.

It is easy to appreciate that quantitative research will entail some amount of data collection. This is because a lot of numbers are generated, collated and analyzed mathematically or statistically. In qualitative research, although words are used more often than numbers, it does not mean that there is no data collection. In fact, data will likely be in the form of observations, ideas, opinions, etc. Like quantitative data, such qualitative data will form the basis for analysis in qualitative research.

4.8 What is a case study?

A case study might be conducted as research during for a PW. In fact, it is apt to be done as a PW and as part of an internship when a student is attached with a company. Adelman *et al.* describe the case study as an 'instance in action' or 'bounded system' (cited in Nunan, 2005: 75–76). Specifically, a case study is meant to provide a holistic narrative of a phenomenon with a debut, middle and conclusion. The following definition of a 'case study' from Merriam (1988: 16) is poignant for this type of research:

> 'The qualitative case study can be defined as an intensive, holistic description and analysis of a single entity, phenomenon or social unit. Case studies are particularistic, descriptive and heuristic and rely heavily on inductive reasoning in handling multiple data sources'.

In addition as Nunan (2005: 74) states, a case study often applies a range of methods for collecting and analyzing data. So it is generally viewed as a 'methodological hybrid'.

This type of inquiry is often a part of 'action research', which is a term originally coined by Lewin (1946). This kind of research involves comparative investigations on the conditions and effects of various forms of social action.

In order for this to be accomplished, the researcher is required to conduct a case study or a series of several case studies involving a 'spiral of steps, each of which is composed of a circle of planning, action and fact-finding about the result of the action' (Lewin, 1946: 37). During these iterations, the

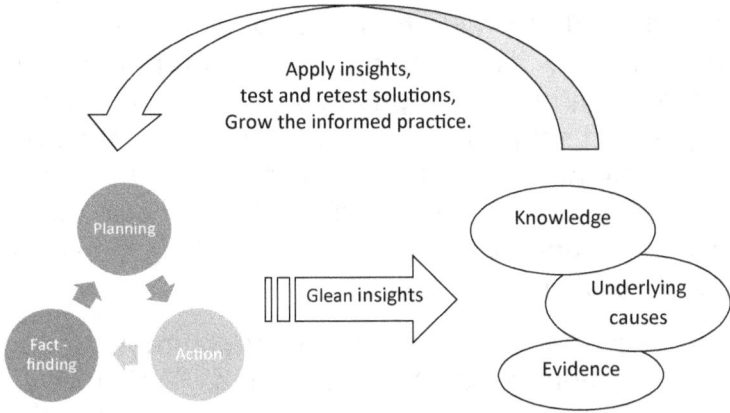

Figure 4.8 Interactive cycles of action research.

researcher will collate evidence, observe underlying causes and construct knowledge. The results from such insights may lead to predictions about potential solutions. These are then applied and their consequences observed making a constantly refined and growing informed practice.

Chandler and Torbert (2003) state that this type of research shares characteristics with experimentation as it involves hypothesis forming followed by testing, evaluating and reporting outcomes. However, unlike scientific enquiry, action research and case study are not focused on statistical findings; they do not place a strong emphasis on objectivity either. For this reason, many claim that validity and reliability are problematic in these processes.

4.9 How to do interview in data collection?

Interview is probably the most common method of data collection in qualitative methodology. This can in turn be further broken down into three major categories: structured; semi-structured and unstructured.

— Structured interview is the most planned and systematic method used; it is akin to a face-to-face survey with fixed questions. No clarification, restructuring, prompting or spontaneous questioning is allowed unless it is part of a pre-planned script. A structured interview does not allow for deviations as wording should always be exactly the same for each interview conducted. Otherwise, other variables might encroach on the results making the study invalid and unreliable.

— Semi-structured interview is a very common strategy for data collection in qualitative research. Similar to a structured interview, this method requires the interviewer to initiate and maintain interaction through questioning and prompting. The interviewer may also react to the interviewees' responses and ask questions in a different order than the planned research design. This allows for more to-and-fro interaction.

— In an unstructured interview, there is no such emphasis on the interviewer–interviewee structure although these social roles are still implicitly present. Interaction is therefore freer flowing and it is not uncommon for the interviewee to initiate some of the conversation. As part of the research design, there may be pre-planned questions and prompts but these are not necessary.

An experienced semi or unstructured interviewer should strive to:

— Ask clear, concise questions;

— Conduct active listening using appropriate body language;

— Respond to *markers* or other keywords brought up during interaction;

— Apply suitable follow-on prompts or questions to elicit detail or explication.

4.10 How to do observation in data collection?

Direct and participant observations are also methods of data collection in qualitative research. What is important is that they involve a close but detached, neutral examination of a natural setting.

Very often what is written is typically called *jot notes. These may be just* key words or terms, short phrases, or even diagrams that will help to describe the phenomenon. In addition, a structured protocol or a rating scale developed prior to the start of the data collection may also be used.

Often, video or photographic techniques are included. One common strategy before an interview is to observe, take photographs and then use these to elicit answers from the interviewee. This is called photo-elicitation.

When more time is available (but as soon as it is possible), these notes may be elaborated upon to become field notes.

Participant observation occurs when a researcher enters the field of investigation to take part in the routine interactions of the participants. The method originated in the work of social anthropologist Bronisław Malinowski (1929) in Britain.

Three differing levels of involvement are presented in Table 4.3:

Howell (1972) presents four stages common to the research process for the active participant observer-researcher. These are: establishing rapport; in the field; recording observations; and analyzing data. When a rapport has been established with the 'subjects' the researcher should strive to blend into the environment and to use reflexive techniques such as a journal to the observations in neutral observational notes. The researcher is encouraged to consider personal factors such as ethnicity, gender or class that may cause subjectivity

Table 4.3 Levels of involvement in participant observations.

Participant observation	Level of Involvement
Moderate	The researcher takes on an "insider" and "outsider" perspective
Active	The researcher becomes a member of the group and takes on its values and behavior to develop a complex understanding
Complete	Prior to the research, the researcher was already an active member.

in the data collection or analysis processes and have an impact on the results of the research.

This impact can have serious consequences on the internal validity of the research. Participant observation can prove to be limited because of the *observer-expectancy effect* also known as *expectancy bias* or the *observer effect*. This posits that the researcher may subconsciously bias the participants and influence the results. Another problem is *confirmation bias* whereby a researcher may interpret the results from an experiment that confirms a hypothesis. This could lead to important information being left out from the report.

4.11 What is coding?

As discussed earlier, qualitative research methods like interviews involve the collection of a lot of information which is generally not as structured. It is necessary to classify, sort and arrange the information collected so as to identify themes, glean insight and develop meaningful conclusions. Codes in the form of a word or a phrase are assigned to such collated and sorted information. This process is called coding. Coding can be conducted based on observations of the occurrence of the words in the transcripts in various patterns. Some of the most common are:

— Sequence;

— Frequency;

— Causation;

— Similarity;

— Difference.

Coding can be a laborious and time intensive exercise. There is however computer software which helps to make this task a lot faster and more accurate. One of these computer programs is NVivo. It must however be emphasized that the computer software is not able to do the thinking. What it does is to provide a platform and tools to enable the students to easily work with the data more easily and efficiently.

Reference: http://www.qsrinternational.com/product

4.12 What is SWOT analysis?

This is a structured planning method used to evaluate the Strengths, Weaknesses, Opportunities, and Threats of a project or a business venture. Thus, SWOT analysis is one of the most commonly used in PW that involves the evaluation of a project, a strategy or a business plan.

Essentially, it involves systematic listing of the insights in a table as shown in Table 4.4.

In the discussion of the SWOT, the information to be collected can either be qualitative or quantitative. Relevant financial and operational ratios can also be included.

Table 4.5 shows a potential extension of the use of the SWOT analysis for strategic planning. Essentially, it leverages on the findings from the SWOT analysis to develop strategies for implementation.

Table 4.4 SWOT analysis.

	Helpful	Harmful
Internal	Strengths: characteristics of the business or project that give it an advantage over others	Weaknesses: characteristics that place the team at a disadvantage relative to others
External	Opportunities: elements that the project could exploit to its advantage	Threats: elements in the environment that could cause trouble for the business or project.

Table 4.5 SWOT strategic table.

	Strengths	Weaknesses
Opportunities	S–O strategies	W–O strategies
Threats	S–T strategies	W–T strategies

Filling up the SWOT analysis as well as the SWOT strategic table can be easy. But, the essence of using this methodology is not filling up the tables themselves. Rather, this method allows the analyst (the students doing the PW in this case) to discuss the otherwise complex competitive and internal issues within a structured framework.

SWOT analysis can be used in conjunction with Focus Group Discussions (FGD). In this instance, participants invited to the FGD can be facilitated to discuss and provide input to fill up the tables in the SWOT analysis.

Please refer to Businessballs (2016) for more information on SWOT analysis.

4.13 What is the Boston Consulting Group Matrix

The Boston Consulting Group (BCG) Matrix is frequently employed to discuss and prioritize different strategies that may be employed in a business for the various products the business is marketing.

Examples:

— A shop selling apparels wants to decide how it should prioritize amongst formal business suits, casual or sports apparels.
— A College would like to decide how it should prioritize the courses it should offer for the different disciplines, such as business, language, information technology engineering, etc.

Figure 4.9 Template for constructing a Boston Consulting Group (BCG) matrix.

This method provides a template for the various products to be categorized and accorded the corresponding treatment (Quick MBA 2010):

4.14 What is reliability and validity and how are these terms viewed in qualitative research methodology?

Assessment of the reliability and validity of qualitative research can bring up problematic issues (Hammersley and Atkinson, 1995; Lincoln and Guba, 1985). Reliability refers to measurement consistency. If a very similar research project was repeated and produced very similar results, it is said to be reliable. Validity can be broken down into two: internal and external validity. External validity questions whether the results from research can be generalized to act as a reflection of a much larger population. Internal validity questions whether results obtained are due to the independent variables from the study and no other causes (*ibid.*).

Action research and case studies are different in nature to experimental research as they do not tend to seek external validity through large scale representative samples; neither do they strive to focus on finite independent variables. Rather, as already stated, they tend to focus on holistic analyses of social phenomena. Therefore notions of reliability and validity are different in these areas of qualitative research. Lincoln and Guba (1985) present the meta-construct 'trustworthiness' to supplant these terms. They put forward four constructs as listed below which can be used by students to check the issue of reliability and validity in their PW. These dimensions are particularly useful in the discussion and conclusion chapters of the PW reports.

a. Credibility: the plausibility and integrity of a study.

b. Transferability: whether results might be applied to other contexts than the research setting.

c. Dependability: where research processes are clearly defined and open to scrutiny.

d. Confirmability: where the outcomes of the study are demonstrably drawn from the data.

CHAPTER 5
ASSESSMENT

After reading this chapter, you will be able to:

— *Determine how formative and summative assessments can be incorporated into Project Work (PW).*

— *Understand how assessments for projects can be structured with multiple assessors including those from the industry.*

— *Familiarize with the poster and 'Pecha Kucha' presentation formats.*

5.1 What is the difference between formative and summative assessment?

Commonly a distinction is made between formative and summative assessment.

Formative assessment is the ongoing process of monitoring and giving feedback on student learning throughout the duration of project work. Marks may be awarded for progress reports submitted by the student, or presentations by the student during the regular project meetings between the supervisor and student.

In contrast, summative assessment is the evaluation of completed project work. Marks may be awarded for the final report submitted by the student or the final presentation by the student.

5.2 How can students participate in formative peer assessment?

Peer review as the name suggests, is feedback and review given by one student to another. When done properly, peer reviews can be very beneficial to both the reviewers and the students being reviewed.

How can peer reviews be organized?

This can be done as part of the regular project meetings between the supervisor and the students. During such meetings, each of the students can take turn to be given some time to present the progress of their work, answer questions or respond to comments from their fellow students.

During peer reviews, students who are performing the role as the reviewers should aim to provide balanced feedback and comments. Some guidelines or 'rules of engagement' for participating in peer review sessions are suggested below:

— Firstly, they can point out the strengths.

— Thereafter, they can raise the problematic areas for discussion or offer suggestions for improvements.

— Rather than just general comments, the comments should refer to specific examples.

— Be respectful and constructive. The objective is not to find fault with another student, but to identify what can be done better so that both the reviewer and the student being reviewed can learn together.

What to observe and what questions to ask in peer reviews? Some suggestions for these are given below. These are some common issues that an audience would like to understand from a project presentation, be it from the perspective of a supervisor, assessor, or a fellow student. Hence, these are the same dimensions the students who are being reviewed or assessed should also bear in mind.

a. Topic and empirical data

— Is the topic relevant? Is the project filling a gap in current knowledge?

— Do the data analyses and/or textual analyses relate well to the research questions?

— Does the Literature review cite and analyze current literature, research and findings from the field?

b. Conceptual framework

— Is the conceptual framework appropriate for the project?

— Are key concepts defined suitably and used consistently?

- Is the conceptual framework applied effectively?
- Is the Literature review relevant? How does the literature review inform the formulation of the conceptual framework?

c. Logical reasoning
- Is the reasoning cogent?
- Is empirical evidence (data, texts, sources) applied effectively?
- Are the limitations of the findings appropriately stated?

d. Implication/application of research
- Is the relevance of the findings clear?
- Is there a contribution of new knowledge?

e. Communicative effectiveness
- Is the focus of the report clearly stated (e.g., the purpose, problem, objectives; the research questions; and the theoretical underpinning)?
- Is the author's expression coherent?
- Is the writing appropriate?

5.3 How should summative assessment be conducted?

This is a very big topic. Every institution will have their respective policies. In any case, this will entail at least the following key considerations:

a. What proportion of the score should be taken from the supervisor and examiner respectively?

b. The number of examiners to be provided. While having more than one examiner will help to reduces bias, this will increase the manpower required.

c. In the case of industry-based PW, there will also be a further question of whether the industry collaborator should also contribute to the assessment?

Table 5.1 provides an example of how the assessment framework can be structured. A component of 'Conduct' is included in this example. This is because it is important to emphasize not just the final outcome of the project, but also how the PW is conducted. Hopefully, this will motivate students to embrace the discipline necessary to carry out the PW properly.

In the example in Table 5.1, the weight of the scores is distributed equally between the Supervisor and the Examiners based on the consideration that both parties are professionals and will uphold the ethics and professionalism in providing an objective assessment. A not insignificant weight is also given to the academic supervisor so as to provide additional levers for him or her to influence the behavior of the students in carrying out the project.

In addition to the apportionment of the scores amongst the supervisors and the examiners, there is also a further consideration of what to assess. An example of a rubric that may be used by the supervisor and examiners for the content component of the assessment is discussed in Table 5.2. Notice that the way this is structured is still based on the key stages in the process of enquiry (i.e., Introduction, literature review, methodology, results and conclusion). However, some of them have been clustered into three main assessment components to allow more flexibility in case the structure of the report does not correspond exactly to the five stages in the process of inquiry.

Table 5.1 Assessment rubric.

Components		Weight	Remarks
Conduct	Academic Supervisor	20%	Rubric: a. Attendance and punctuality at project meetings. b. Professionalism in conduct. c. Engagements with substantive matter relating to the project. d. Adherence to periodic milestone submissions. e. Contribution, teamwork, and leadership (if it is a group project).
Content	Academic Supervisor	30%	In industry-based PWs, the industry collaborator can be considered to be included in the assessment also. One way of doing this is to assign some weight of his assessment from the component of the academic supervisor. The quantum will depend on the level of direct involvement in his supervision on the PW. As assessment for PW is primarily for partial fulfilment of a curricular requirement, the weight of the academic supervisor should carry the majority, say, not less than 50% of this component. Alternatively, this component may still be entered by the academic supervisor alone. However, he or she may consult and seek the industry supervisor's input when doing so.
	Examiner or Assessor	50%	If there is more than one examiner, this can be apportioned among them equally.

Table 5.2 Academic Supervisor's and Examiner's rubric.

Components	Weight	Descriptions
Format, Aesthetics, Language and Structure (FALS) Key source chapters: The entire report.	20%	a. Organized and logical structure. b. Adherence to a consistent format and referencing style, such as APA, the styles of mainstream journals, or other styles in line with professional practice. c. Reasonable fluency and accuracy of the language used.
Framing Key source chapters: Introduction, Literature review, Methodology.	40%	a. Clear articulation of the objectives. b. Appropriateness of the literature reviewed and pertinence of the critique. c. Ability to link the literature reviewed to identify the knowledge gap and construct an appropriate conceptual framework of research. d. Good discussion on the methodology employed and the rationale.
Results and Analysis Key source chapters: Results, Conclusion.	40%	a. Ability to present the data collected meaningfully. b. Appropriate analyses consistent with the stated methodology. c. Appropriate discussions of the findings and limitations. d. Recommendation for potential application in practice or future further inquiry.

In the example above, equal weight is assigned to 'Framing' as well as 'Results and Analysis' to align with the twin curricular objectives of project-based learning as discussed in Section 1.3.

5.4 Does the assessment rubric need to be different for research-based and practice-based projects respectively?

The fundamental guiding principle is that regardless of whether the project is research or practice based, the approach to solving problems will still entail the stages of enquiry:

a. Introduction,

b. Literature review,

c. Methodology,

d. Analysis,

e. Conclusions.

While the Literature review is quite commonly understood for research-based projects, there is some contention on whether it is relevant or needed for practice-based projects.

As discussed in the earlier section on the Literature review, for practice-based projects, Literature review can be regarded as situation analysis or an extended discussion on the definition of the problem to be solved in the project. The reference sources for the literature review in such practice-based projects can be more encompassing to include periodicals published by professional bodies, reports in various media channels, reports and proprietary papers pertaining to the hosting of industry clients, etc.

Thus, as long as such 'calibration' is explicitly put forth for common understanding by the students, supervisors and assessor, the assessment rubric as described in Table 5.2 should still be applicable for both research-based and practice-based projects. In any case, the clustering of the five stages of inquiry into three main clusters as shown in Table 5.2 would have provided some flexibility and addressed the concerns some may have.

5.5 What is a poster presentation and how to prepare for this?

Poster presentation may be used in the following ways:

— As an additional component in the assessment of projects.

— As an alternative channel of presentation in an academic or professional conference, i.e., *in-lieu* of the oral presentation of the full paper.

A common way poster presentations are organized is that posters will be displayed in a room or an exhibition hall. There will be time slots where the authors will have to stand next to their posters whereby judges, examinations and/or the general audience will come to view their posters and seek clarifications on their own time within the schedules given.

As in the case of the PW reports, each institution or journal may stipulate their own requirements or specifications. Generally, the size of the posters is stipulated to be A0 size (84 cm × 118 cm).

Checklist for the design of posters:

a. Due to the nature of poster presentation, the content of the poster should by and large be self-explanatory. It should communicate the essence of the project.

b. Arrange the content in a simple and uncluttered manner. If you find you have too much content to present, it is likely

Figure 5.3 Poster presentation in a conference.

that you have to review and prioritize. It is not expected nor is it feasible to include all the findings of your project within a poster. The purpose of the poster is to highlight the key aspects of the project only. Where details are needed, the audience can be directed to read the full report.

c. The headings or key sections of the content should correspond with that of the PW report; for example: objective, background, methodology, results and conclusions.

d. The information and findings presented in the poster should correspond with the full report. Indeed, a common mistake seen in the works of students is that the information presented in the posters does not correspond with the full report. This is not only embarrassing. It may reflect sloppiness or weaknesses in the thought process.

One possible reason for this is that students only work on the posters in the last minute and worse still, after they have finalized or even submitted the full report. While working on the posters, they may come across new content or gain new perspectives. Thus, it is advisable to bear in mind the content of the poster in conjunction with the writing of the PW report throughout the duration of the project.

Reminder: do not leave the poster to the last minute.

e. The text should be brief. It is fine to write in bullet form.

f. The text should be readable for the audience who will likely be reading it from a distance of about 1 to 2 m. A font size of at least 30 point is recommended. This includes text in charts and diagrammes. Fonts of headings should be correspondingly larger.

g. Use simple and clear font such as Arial or Calibri. Minimize the use of different types of font. If necessary, use at most two types of fonts.

h. Use consistent font type and font size for similar type of text. For example, if Calibri size 40 is used for headings, then all headings should use Calibri size 40.

i. Ensure the color of the text and the background is of sufficient contrast so that the text is legible.

j. Make good use of charts and diagrams to optimize the visual impact. If there is a conceptual framework of analysis, this should be central to the design of the poster.

5.6 What is the 'Pecha Kucha' presentation format?

The 'Pecha Kucha' presentation format was started amongst the design and creative community in Tokyo in 2003. The name 'Pecha Kucha' is derived from the Japanese word for chit chat. Specifically, it was introduced by the firm Klein Dytham Architecture for the sharing of design ideas and creative works (Pecha Kucha, 2016). The presentations were done in 'Pecha Kucha Nights' that have since spread all over the world.

The 'Pecha Kucha' presentation format is gaining popularity for use in professional and academic conferences. It is also very suitable to be used for class presentations by groups of students. In PW, it can be considered as a format for students to provide periodic updates on their progress and interim findings, and/or as an alternative to poster presentation which may form one of the components of the assessment for PW.

In essence, the 'Pecha Kucha' presentation format contains the following features:

— Maximum of 20 slides.
— Each slide is set to advance after 20 s.
— As a result, the total presentation will last 6 min and 40 s exactly.

The key advantage of 'Pecha Kucha' format over the normal presentations is that there are fixed durations for each slide and the total presentation. As a result, the presenters are motivated to move along with the messages they want to deliver within the time given. For the organizers of the presentations or the assessors if this format is to be used in an assessment, it is easier for them to plan the overall schedules of the event.

Compared with a poster presentation, the 'Pecha Kucha' format is able to show more information as it has the 'space' of 20 slides to do so instead of a single poster. However, the slides need to be accompanied by narration.

A point of clarification: We are not suggesting that 'Pecha Kucha' presentation or for that matter any other forms of presentations can be used as a sole format of assessment. These

Table 5.3 Comparison of the different presentation formats.

	Normal PowerPoint presentation	Poster presentation	Pecha Kucha presentation
Number of slides.	Not fixed.	One poster of a specific dimension. Normally set as A size (84 cm × 118 cm)	20 slides.
Dwell time of each slide.	Not fixed.	N.A.	20 s.
Total duration.	Not fixed.	Not fixed.	6 min and 40 s.
Must it be accompanied by narration?	Yes.	Not necessary. But, time slots may be allocated for authors to stand by the posters to answer questions as may be needed by the visitors.	Yes.
Can it be self-explanatory?	Possible to some extent.	Possible. It can be exhibited as a static display.	Unlikely, as the slides are likely to consist of mainly images with little text.

are usually complements, to be used alongside the submission and assessment of the formal reports or dissertations.

Some tips for making good 'Pecha Kucha' presentations

— As the dwell time for each slide is only 20 s, there is little time for the audience to read the texts on the slides if they are too wordy. Thus, make good use of images to communicate the information and ideas. These images can also be in the form of charts and tables.

— Use text sparingly and selectively. For example, display key words or key phrases only.

— Write the script for the oral narration. Rehearse the oral narration in conjunction with the advancement of the slides in 20 s intervals. The use of key words in the slides may help to provide useful reminders. If you are using PowerPoint, you can also write the script on the note pane.

— Although time available for the presentation is constrained, there is no need to rush. It is more important to provide fewer details, but more pertinent information at the level of granulation suitable for the context.

CHAPTER 6
PROJECT MANAGEMENT

After reading this chapter, you will be able to:

— *Set up a plan for effective management of a project.*

— *Design a series of related projects that span over multiple semesters.*

6.1 Is it necessary for interim reports to be submitted in addition to the final report? If these are needed, how can these be organized?

Usually, a PW will last at least a semester to a year. Interim submissions spaced out over the duration of the PW are recommended. They will help the supervisors and students to monitor the progress of the PW, review feedback and make adjustments as may be needed.

One way of designing the interim submissions may be to structure them as drafts of the various chapters of the dissertation, based on which interim feedback may be given to the students. An example is shown in Table 6.1:

6.2 Is it necessary for PW to have regular scheduled project meetings?

While PW forms part of the curriculum, it differs from the other regularly taught modules in not having scheduled classes.

Table 6.1 Milestones for the submission of interim reports.

Submission	Content	Timeline (Assuming the PW is to be completed within a semester of 14 weeks.)
1st	Chapter 1 Introduction, and Chapter 2 Literature Review.	By week 4
2nd	Chapter 3 Methodology	By week 7.
3rd	Chapter 4 Results, and Chapter 5 Conclusion.	By week 13.

Thus, the Academic Supervisors may need to make direct arrangements to meet the students from time to time.

As PW forms an integral part of the curriculum, it is important that the formal project meetings be pre-arranged. Preferably, the schedules of such meetings need to be organized at the onset of the project. The details such as time, venue, agenda and persons required to attend at each meeting should be itemized explicitly as far as possible. This will help the supervisors and students to commit to a set of milestones.

Where feasible, it is also recommended that the academic institution may build into the formal time-table for periodic (weekly, fortnightly or any other appropriate intervals) project meetings. This will go a long way for the supervisors and students to have 'protected' time slots to discuss the projects.

Please see Annex A for a sample project schedule. It shows how each of the scheduled project meetings can be pre-planned with pre-readings, agenda and follow ups.

6.3 What is a Gantt chart?

Gantt chart is a tool for managing project schedules. A simple Gantt chart done with Microsoft Word is shown Annex C. Students can follow this as a template to develop one for their projects.

Please note some comments below:

— In order to avoid a last minute rush and timely completion of the project, the project schedule needs to be planned as early as possible at the beginning of the project.

— Activities in a project need not necessarily be carried out in discrete sequence. In fact, many activities can be carried out concurrently. For example, students will need to consult the literatures not only for the chapter on literature review. They will also need to do this to develop the chapters on Introduction and Methodology. Finally, when they analyze the results and write the discussions and the conclusion, they may also need to consult the literature to triangulate with other sources of information and critically discuss the findings. Please see Section 2.1 also.

— In some institutions, PWs are stipulated to be completed within one semester, which will typically last about 13 to 16 weeks. This is a very tight timeframe. Thus, some institutions will arrange for the proposal and allocation to be carried out before the start of the semester. On the other hand, for projects that are meant to be completed over an academic year, there will be more leeway for the project proposal stage to commence only at the start of the academic year.

More sophisticated Gantt charts can be developed with Microsoft Excel or the specialized project management software Microsoft Project. In particular Microsoft Project can be used to conduct critical path analysis, which is to determine if and how a project is delayed, what causes the delays and how the situation can be remedied. However, it is unlikely that this level of sophistication and complexity is required for the purpose of managing PW.

However, if the substantive matter of the PW is regarding project management, such as to determine the critical path for the planning and organizing the Olympic Games, then it will be worthwhile to consider the use of such specialized software as part of the methodology. Students can read more about this in Microsoft (2016).

6.4 What if the project is too big and it cannot be structured within one PW and be completed in a Semester or an Academic Year?

Sometimes, a project is too big. It cannot be structured within one PW to be completed in a semester or an academic year. In such instances, the academic supervisor will have to design an overarching 'programme', which may encompass several PW to be completed by a few PW teams, over a few semesters or academic years.

Accordingly, the academic supervisor will have to be more involved in connecting the sub-components to form a larger whole. It is also possible that such an over-arching program is set within the context of an industry-linked project that is commissioned by an industry partner towards addressing a problem in practice. This may also be a research program the academic supervisor is pursuing with the intention of putting together one or a series of related academic papers for publication.

Table 6.2 shows an example of how this can be done schematically. In this case, the over-arching program is designed to last over four phases from Phase A to D. The duration of each of these phases is equivalent to one academic semester. In Phase A, the scope of the PW may be directed at developing a survey instrument, conducting preliminary data collection and testing its validity. In Phase B, the scope may include actual data collection and collation. In Phase C, the scope may be focused on analysis. In Phase D, the work may be done primarily by the academic staff and may not involve students in PW.

Although students involved in each of Phases A to D mentioned above may only be involved in certain aspects of the overall overarching programme, their learning experience need not be compromised. In fact, for students involved in earlier phase(s) of the study, they can learn to ensure their work will be useful input for further investigation in subsequent phases. Likewise, for students involved in later phase(s) of the study, they will learn how to take the work done in the earlier phase(s) as secondary data for their portion of the study.

If such a program is commissioned by an industry partner, student internships may also be leveraged upon to contribute to the program. Similar to PWs, student internships are also organized in accordance with the academic semesters. During the internships, students are attached to the industry partner on a full-time basis for the duration of the semester. The industry partner who hosts interns may assign the interns with roles such as project management or other tasks envisaged in the internship.

While Table 6.2 shows a program that lasts two academic years encompassing four semesters, smaller or larger programs lasting two or more semesters can also be structured.

6.5 Can a project be assigned to more than one candidate or groups of students?

This is possible. Indeed, this can be an approach to coordinate several candidates to work on a large scale project.

For example, a project is commissioned by the Singapore National Olympic Council to develop a venue strategy to host the Asian Games. Assuming that the Asian Games comprises 32 sports, the eventual deliverable of the project will be to present a recommendation on where each of the sports can be held. Some sports will likely be able to be held at existing

Table 6.2 How a combination of Commissioned Project, Internship and PW may be structured.

Phases of the over-arching Programme	Timing	Scope of the PW	Student Internship
A	Semester 1, April 2018 to August 2018	Designing the survey instrument and testing its validity	Project Management
B	Semester 2, October 2018 to February 2019	Data Collection and collation	Project Management
C	Semester 1, April 2019 to August 2019	Analysis	Project Management
D	Semester 2, October 2019 to February 2019	No PW is involved. Synthesis of the entire project into an integrated project report by the staff	Project Management

venues. For others, temporary or new permanent venues may need to be erected.

However, to study the venues for all the 32 sports, the scope will be too large to be included within a single project to be completed by a single candidate. One way to organize this is to assign the project to several candidates. In this case, four candidates can be assigned to this project whereby each candidate can evaluate the venue strategy for eight sports.

The four candidates can collaborate to co-develop the conceptual framework and jointly select the methodology. They can also collaborate in coordinating meetings, engaging clients, and jointly manage the data collection effort. However, they will have to write their reports individually for separate submissions.

Please see Annex B for a sample project proposal which describes this scenario. It is written from the perspective of the academic supervisor to recruit students for the project.

CHAPTER 7
ETHICS DECLARATION

After reading this chapter, you will be able to:

— *Understand the rationale and requirements of an ethics declaration.*

— *Perform an ethics declaration in accordance to the requirements of the institution concerned.*

7.1 Why is there a need to declare 'ethics' in research or project work?

The requirement for an ethics declaration in scientific and social science research is still evolving. In recent history, there were two incidents that provided the impetus to this heightened consciousness of the need to address the issue of ethics in research. Specifically, this is to protect human subjects or the samples from being used as 'guinea pigs' in research.

In the first example, human beings were used as subjects for research by the Nazis in Germany during the Second World War. In the second example, known effective treatment for syphilis was withheld from African–American participants who were infected with syphilis in a study. These practices are considered unethical.

Since then, researchers and the academia have become more sensitized to the need to protect participants in research projects. Protocols and standards have been developed to serve this need. Where the nature of the PW is research, it is necessary for those involved to acquaint themselves with this subject matter.

7.2 What are the key principles to consider in administering ethics?

The key objective of administering ethics in research is to protect the privacy, rights and well-being of research participants as the subjects. Accordingly, the following principles can be referred to as a guide:

a. Voluntary participation — People should not be compelled to participate in the research as a subject. This is especially important if the proposed subjects are 'captive audiences' in the sense that they may feel that they have little or no choice to opt out. For example, students of the researchers, subordinates of the researchers, patients in hospitals, prisoners, staff of a company, members of a club, etc.

b. Informed consent — The prospective research participants must be fully informed about the procedures, duration involved, and risks involved in the research. They must be given the choice to provide their consent to participate voluntarily. They may do so by filling out an informed consent form. In addition, the participants should not be subject to the risks of being injured or harmed psychologically or physically during the research. At no time should they feel they are compelled to participate.

c. Protection of privacy by guarantee of confidentiality — Participants should be assured that information about their identity will not be made available to anyone who is not directly involved in the study. Even for those involved in the research who have access to the identity or particulars of the participants, such information should not be used for anything else other than the intended research.

d. Protection of privacy by guarantee of anonymity — This is a stricter standard than confidentiality. Essentially, this means that the participant will remain anonymous throughout the study — even to the researchers themselves.

The administration of ethics in research is normally done by an Institutional Review Board (IRB) set up within an institution. This IRB is a panel which may comprise experts in science, law, education, research protocols. Their primary responsibility is to evaluate project proposals with respect to potential implications on ethics.

The review panel may decide to approve the project proposal as it is or they may reject it. More commonly, where the project proposal is found to have insufficient provisions for compliance with the requirements for ethics, the IRB will usually make recommendations for additional actions to be taken so that the requirements for the safeguarding of the safety and rights of participants are met.

By reviewing proposals for research, IRB helps to protect both the organization and the researcher against potential legal implications of neglecting to address important ethical issues of participants.

Reference: http://www.socialresearchmethods.net/kb/ethics.php

7.3 Do the requirements for the declaration of ethics differ in different institutions and in different countries?

Generally, different institutions will have different requirements and protocols for the administration of an 'ethics declaration'. Having said that, they should all subscribe to the same principles as discussed in Section 7.2.

7.4 Is there any situation when an ethics declaration is not required?

Generally, research which involves the use of human subjects will need to go through a thorough review of the protocols to ensure the stipulated ethical standards are adhered to.

In contrast, economics and engineering studies which do not involve the use of human subjects will likely be waived of the requirements of going through the entire ethics declaration process. Usually, an accelerated process involving only a declaration that the study does not involve the use of human subjects may suffice.

7.5 What does the process for ethics declaration entail?

The administration of an ethics declaration can involve a fair amount of effort and the completion of some documents. It is good to start this early. Every institution will have its own requirements and process. Where there are national laws governing such matters, the regulations that are introduced by the respective educational or research institutions are required to align with them.

In Singapore, the Human Biomedical Research Act was passed in Parliament in August 2015. This law includes criminally enforceable requirements for consent, the formation of the Institution Review Board (IRB), the administration of the procedures as well as the requirements for record keeping. It also spells out clearly the responsibilities of the researcher, the IRB, and the institutions concerned.

It is therefore important for the academic and industry supervisors involved in projects relating to human biomedical research to familiarize and comply with these regulatory requirements. Sufficient time should be set aside during the design phase of the project to ensure all the requirements and procedures are complied with. It is not unusual for the procedures to take a few months or even to exceed a year for complex cases that may entail several cycles of submission and resubmissions.

Bangor University (2016) provides a comprehensive description of the procedures as well as forms used in the process.

BIBLIOGRAPHY

American Psychological Association [APA] (2016). Available at: http://www.apastyle.org/.

An Example of a Hypothesis Test. (2016). Available at: http://statistics.about.com/od/Inferential-Statistics/a/An-Example-Of-A-Hypothesis-Test.htm.

Analytics Vidhya (2016). Your guide to master hypothesis testing in statistics. Available at: http://www.analyticsvidhya.com/blog/2015/09/hypothesis-testing-explained/.

Bangor University. (2016). *Ethics*. Available at: https://www.bangor.ac.uk/cbless/ethics.php.en.

Berman, J. (2008). Connecting with industry: Bridging the divide. *Journal Of Higher Education Policy & Management*, 30(2), 165–174.

Burges, T. F. (2001). *A General Introduction to the Design of Questionnaires for Survey Research*. University of Leeds. Available at: http://iss.leeds.ac.uk/downloads/top2.pdf.

Businessballs. (2016). *SWOT analysis*. Available at: http://www.businessballs.com/swotanalysisfreetemplate.htm.

Buzan, T. (2013). *Mind Map Handbook: The Ultimate Thinking Tool*. HarperCollins, UK.

Cavana, R. Y., Delahaye, B. L., & Sekaran, U. (2001). *Applied Business Research: Qualitative and Quantitative Methods*. John Wiley & Sons, Australia.

Chandler, D., & Torbert, B. (2003). Transforming inquiry and action interweaving 27 flavors of action research. *Action Research*, 1(2), 133–152.

Creative Research Systems. (2016). *Sample Size Calculator*. Available at: http://www.surveysystem.com/sscalc.htm.

Daekin University. (2015). *Harvard — Daekin University Guide to Referencing*. Available at: http://www.deakin.edu.au/students/study-support/referencing/harvard.

de Kock, M. (2015). Ontology and a mixed methods epistemology in applied research. *Proceedings Of The European Conference On E-Learning*, 170–176.

Emmitt, M., & Pollock, J. (1997). *Language and Learning. An introduction for Teaching*. 2nd edition. Oxford: University Press, Oxford.

English Language Roots. (2016) Available at: http://www.prefixsuffix.com/rootchart.php.

Forbes (2014). A Unified Framework For Innovation. Available at: http://www.forbes.com/sites/reuvencohen/2014/03/31/design-thinking-a-unified-framework-for-innovation/#35b2f03a56fc. Accessed on March 31, 2014.

Grammar (2016). Available at: https://reading.ac.uk/internal/studyadvice/StudyResources/Writing/sta-grammar.aspx.

Halliday, M. H., & Hasan, S. I. R. (1976). *Cohesion in English*. Longman, London.

Hammersley, M., & P. Atkinson (1995). *Ethnography: Principles in Practice*. Routledge, London and New York.

Hendrickson, G. (1954). A Comparison of Theses and Projects. *Journal of Teacher Education,* 5(4), 302–306.

Howell, J. T. (1972). *Hard Living on Clay Street: Portraits of Blue Collar Families*. Waveland Press, Inc, Prospect Heights, Illinois pp. 392–403.

Human Biomedical Research Act. (2015). Republic of Singapore Government Gazette. Available at: http://www.statutes.agc.gov.sg.

IBM (2016a). SPSS Software - Predictive analytics software and solutions. Available at: http://www-01.ibm.com/software/sg/analytics/spss/.

IBM (2016b). SPSS Amos. Available at: http://www-03.ibm.com/software/products/en/spss-amos.

International Baccllaureatte [IB] (2016). Extended Essay. Available at: http://ibo.org/programmes/diploma-programme/curriculum/extended-essay/.

Ithaca College Library (2016). Primary and Secondary Sources. Available at: https://library.ithaca.edu/sp/subjects/primary.

Katamba, F. (2005). *English words: Structure, History, Usage*. Routledge, London.

Krajcik, J. S., & Blumenfeld, P. C. (2006). Project-based learning. In Keith Sawyer, R. (Ed.), *The Cambridge Handbook of the Learning Sciences*. Cambridge University Press, Cambridge, pp. 317–334.

Lake Tahoe Community College [LTCC] (2016). The standard normal distribution. Available at: http://www.ltcconline.net/greenl/courses/201/probdist/zScore.htm.

Lewin, K. (1946). Action research and minority problems. *Journal of Social Issues,* 2(4), 34–46.

Lincoln, Y. S., & Guba, E. G. (1985). *Naturalistic Inquiry.* Sage Publications. Thousand Oaks, CA.

Luke, A., Freebody, P., Shun, L., & Gopinathan, S. (2005). Towards research-based innovation and reform: Singapore schooling in transition. *Asia Pacific Journal of Education,* 25(1), 5–28.

Malinowski, B. (1929). *The sexual life of savages in North-Western Melanesia: An Ethnographic Account of Courtship, Marriage and Family Life Among the Natives of the Trobriand Islands, British New Guinea.* Halcyon House, New York.

Merriam, S. B. (1998). *Qualitative research and Case Study Applications in Education.* Jossey-Bass. San Francisco, CA.

Microsoft. (2016). *Project — Deliver winning projects.* Available at: https://products.office.com/en-us/project/project-and-portfolio-management-software.

Ministry of Education, Singapore [MOE] (2016). Integrated Programmes. Available at: https://www.moe.gov.sg/education/secondary/other/integrated-programme/.

Nunan, D. (2005). Classroom research. *Handbook of Research in Second Language Teaching and Learning.* Lawrence Erlbaum Mahwah, NJ, pp. 225–240.

Office of National Statistics. (2016). What is qualitative research? Available at: http://www.ons.gov.uk/ons/guide-method/method-quality/general-methodology/data-collection-methodology/what-is-qualitative-research-/index.html.

Pecha Kucha (2016). Available at: http://www.pechakucha.org/faq.

Purdue University. (2016). Purdue Online Writing Lab. Available at: https://owl.english.purdue.edu/owl/resource/560/01/.

Quick MBA (2010). Available at: http://www.quickmba.com/.

Root word lesson (2016). Available at: https://myvocabulary.com/dir-root-root_master.

Simons, L., Fehr, L., Blank, N., Connell, H., Georganas, D., Fernandez, D., & Peterson, V. (2012). Lessons learned from experiential learning: what do students learn from a practicum/internship? *International Journal Of Teaching & Learning In Higher Education,* 24(3), 325–334.

Simon, H. (1969). *The Sciences of the Artificial.* Cambridge, MA.
Teng, A. (2014). Singapore comes out tops for the fourth year in International Baccalaureate exams. T*he Straits Times*, Singapore, January 6, 2014. Available at: http://www.straitstimes.com/singapore/singapore-comes-out-tops-for-the-fourth-year-in-international-baccalaureate-exams.
Thomas, J. W. (2000). *A Review of Research on Project-Based Learning.* Available at: http://bie.org/index.php/site/RE/pbl_research/29.
Trochim, M.K. (2006). What is the Research Methods Knowledge Base. Available at: http://www.socialresearchmethods.net/kb/index.php.
University of Illinois (2016). Writing a Research Proposal. Available at: http://www.library.illinois.edu/learn/research/proposal.html.
Walliman, N. (2011). *Your Research Project: Designing and Planning Your Work.* Sage Publications, Thousand Oaks, CA.

ANNEX A
PROJECT SCHEDULE

An example of a schedule of project meetings between the supervisors and the students is shown below. The timeline shown is based on a project to be completed within a 14-week semester. Whilst only five meetings are shown in this illustration, more intermediate meetings may be scheduled where needed. In addition, it is likely that the students will need to schedule further working meetings amongst themselves.

Meetings	Schedule and deliverable

1st Meeting	— When: By week 1.
	— Pre-reading:
	  — Walliman (2011) or equivalent to familiarize with the research process.
	  — Website of the client.
	  — Each student is to research and present at least two articles from newspapers, magazines, books, or journals on issues relating to the project.
	— Agenda at meeting:
	  — Individual sharing on what they have found out from the pre-readings.
	  — Project Plan and the expectations of the client.
	— Follow up:
	  — Commence drafting Chapter 1 Introduction. Commence sourcing articles and reading them for literature review.
	  — Target to submit the draft of Chapter 1 Introduction and Chapter 2 Literature Review by week 4.

2nd Meeting	— When: By week 3
	— Agenda:
	  — Individual sharing on the follow up from the previous meeting.
	  — Discussion on how to develop the conceptual framework of analysis.
	  — Discussion on the methodology.
	— Follow up:
	  — Formulate the conceptual framework of analysis. Start drafting Chapter 3 Methodology. If the project requires a questionnaire, start developing the questionnaire.
	  — Target to submit the draft of Chapter 3 Methodology and the questionnaire where applicable by week 7.

(*Continued*)

(*Continued*)

Meetings	Schedule and deliverable

3rd Meeting	— When: By week 6.
	— Agenda:
	  — Individual sharing on Chapter 3.
	  — Confirmation of the methodology and the questionnaire where applicable.
	  — Make arrangements for the logistics of data collection.
	— Follow up:
	  — Implement the plan for data collection.

4th Meeting	— When: By week 9.
	— Agenda:
	  — Inspect the data collected.
	  — Discuss issues encountered with analysis.
	— Follow up:
	  — Proceed with data analysis and the drafting of Chapter 4 Results and Chapter 5 Conclusion.

5th Meeting	— When: By week 12.
	— Agenda:
	  — Individual presentation of the draft Chapters 4 and 5.
	— Follow up:
	  — Review the etire report. Do the final editing to ensure that all the chapters flow coherently.
	  — Target to submit the completed final report by Week 14.

ANNEX B

PROJECT PROPOSAL SAMPLE

PROJECT PROPOSAL

Programme of study: Bachelor of Business Administration
Module: Final Year Project
Academic Year: 2017.

1. Title: Strategic venue planning for major international sports events in Singapore.[1]

2. Objectives: The Objective of the project is to develop the venue strategy for the hosting of an international multi-sport event like the Asian Games in Singapore.

3. Is the project industry linked or commissioned by a company or an organization? (Please underline and elaborate accordingly).

	If Yes, please provide the name of the organization and the particulars of the key contact person.
Yes	Organization: Singapore National Olympic Council. Website: www.snoc.org.sg
	Contact person (name, designation, email, phone number): Mr. Andrew Kwong General Manager, Events Development Division. Email: ak@snoc.org.sg. Tel: 65-89765672
No.	

4. Background:

Hosting major international sports events like the Asian Games requires a lot of space. There have been debates about whether Singapore is too small or if the infrastructure is adequate to host major multi-sports international sports event like the Asian Games. The aim of the project

---

[1] The inclusion of 'Singapore' in the title will make it more specific. It helps to communicate the scope of the project.

is therefore to develop venue strategy for the hosting of a major multi-sport event like the Asian Games in Singapore and to demonstrate its feasibility. The planning horizon is 10 years and beyond.[2]

The project will entail, for a start, a proposal for a planning framework for venue selection. Based on the framework thus developed, data collection and analysis can be carried out to include the identification and compilation of the requirements for the venues for the various sports as well as the availability of existing venues for such requirements. Where no existing venues are found suitable, there should also be a proposal on the alternative approach to make available such venues.

The scope of the feasibility evaluation will be confined to identifying venue solutions that meet the technical requirements of the sports concern. Financial feasibility analysis will fall outside of the scope of this study. However, it will be good for this aspect to be reflected in the over-arching planning framework.

The subject matter of the project will be related to the modules of events management, strategic planning and facilities management. There will be opportunity for students to apply the concepts from these modules in an integrated way to develop the solution for the client.

5. Methodology:

    The project is practice-centric. It will employ a mixed methods approach for data collection and analysis. It will entail primarily the collecting and compilation of information from secondary sources.

---

[2]The indication of the planning horizon is intended to communicate the scope of the analysis. In this example, the ten-year planning horizon will allow the development of new venues to be considered.

One of a few focus group discussions among the National Sports Associations may also be organized. A couple of site visits to the venues being evaluated may also be necessary. The client will assist in organizing these.

The discussion should include the analysis of the availability and suitability of the identified venues against a set of criteria to be developed as part of the planning framework.

6. Key sources for literature review:

   The following may be used as the primary reference for the conceptual framework of analysis:

   French, S. P., & Disher, M. E. (1997). Atlanta and the Olympics: A One-year Retrospective. *Journal of the American Planning Association*, 63(3), 379–392.

   Masterman, G. (2014). *Strategic Sports Event Management*. 3rd Edition. Routledge, London.

   Siegfried, J., & Zimbalist, A. (2000). The Economics of Sports Facilities and Their Communities. *The Journal of Economic Perspectives*, 14(3), 95–114.

   The other sources, especially for the technical requirements of the venues will be largely websites of the Singapore National Olympic Council, the Olympic Council of Asia, as well as those of the governing bodies of the various sports concerned.

7. Personnel of the project:

   Academic Supervisor:

   Damien Bush, Lecturer, Faculty of Business. Dr Bush will be the Principal Investigator (PI) for the project.

Industry Supervisor:

Andrew Kwong, Director, Events Development Division, Singapore National Olympic Council. Email: ak@snoc.org.sg. Tel: 65-89765672

Students:

This project will be suitable for students in business programs, especially those who have completed the modules of Events Management, Strategic Management, or Facilities Management.

Four students will be selected to undertake this project. Each student will be assigned to cover eight sports. They will submit their reports individually.

8. Project Schedule:

Activities and milestones	Semester 1 (weeks)							Holidays, 4 weeks	Semester 2 (weeks)						
	0	2	4	6	8	10	12	14		0	2	4	6	8	10	12	14
Start of the Semester.	•															
Project allocation.		•	•													
Confirm schedule.			•	•												
Introduction.			•	•	•											
Literature review.				•	•	•	•									
Methodology.						•	•	•								
Data collection.							•	•		•						
Data analysis.							•			•	•	•				
Compile draft report.												•	•	•		
Submit final report.															•		
Oral presentation.																•	•
Presentation to client.																•	•
Semester ends																	•

9. Budget

Items	Unit cost	Units	Total item cost	Total claimable cost	Remarks
Receptions on Focus Group Discussions	$100	4	$400		By client
Transport allowance for site visits	$60	4 persons	$240	$200	
Purchase of software	$300	1	$300	$300	
Total			$940	$540	

ANNEX C
PROJECT GANTT CHART

Activities and milestones	\-4	\-2	0	2	4	6	8	10	12	14	16	18
Research proposal, ethics declarations	•	•										
Project allocation.		•	•									
Start of the Semester.			•									
1st meeting.			•	•								
Formulate and confirm a project schedule.			•	•								
Work on Introduction.			•	•	•							
Work on literature review.				•	•	•	•	•	•			
2nd meeting.					•							
Work on methodology.				•	•	•						
Data collection.						•	•					
3rd meeting.						•						
Work on data analysis.								•	•	•		
4th meeting.								•				
Compilation of draft report.								•	•	•	•	
5th meeting.									•			
Submission of final report.										•		
Semester ends										•		
Presentation or oral examination.											•	•
Presentation to the client, where applicable.											•	•

EPILOGUE

We have written this book based on our personal experience in collaborating with colleagues and partners from the industry, as well as in supervising students in their project work. We are motivated to do so in the hope that this book will help students find clarifications for doubts they may have, understand the rationale for various requirements for project work, develop interest in research or applied research, and set the foundation for further studies. Likewise, we hope that this book has been useful to industry collaborators and academic supervisors to design industry–academic collaborations through PWs as well as helpful to communicate the requirements of PWs to students.

Nonetheless, it is our desire to improve this book to make it even more useful. We welcome feedback and suggestions from fellow academics, students and industry collaborators. In particular, we would like to invite supervisors to contribute exemplars of assessed students' work. We would like to suggest that as a guide, the exemplars may comprise two parts. The first part is a summary of the PW report condensed to about 1500 words. The second part will be the narrative comments of the supervisor of about 500 words of what was good and what can be improved. We hope to include your contributions in future editions of this book. All contributors will be acknowledged.

Ho Mun Wai
Republic Polytechnic, Singapore
Email: ho_mun_wai@rp.edu.sg

Mark Brooke
National University of Singapore
Email: elcmb@nus.edu.sg